Legacy of Success!

Legacy of Success!

Facts will not stand in the way of Obama's Legacy of robust growth, low unemployment, and balanced budgets!

Alan Beasley

Published in the U.S.A.

ISBN: 978-0-615-67553-4

First Printing: July 2012

Cover design by Alan Beasley

Book design by Alan Beasley

Thank you!

To all my friends and family who encouraged me to put my thoughts down on paper – I say Thank You! I am fully aware that, in some cases, that encouragement was partly to get me to shut up. In my heart, I was just filling in the details that I would research – and assumed none of you had the time (or desire) to dig up; but must want to know about, in order to make "educated" decisions for yourselves and families… ☺

I want to say thank you to all those who assisted me in the process of publishing this book. With the advent of e-publishing, and other online services, I realize it seems that everyone is writing a book nowadays. So thank you for your patience with me throughout the process!

Table of Contents

Forward 9

Good Intentions – Disaster Results 13

Words – Carefully chosen, carefully read! 16

Let's play a game 18

Chapter 1 It may sound "odd" 22

Chapter 2 Tricks, Gimmicks, and Repetition 31

Double Meanings Words 40

Chapter 3 Legacy of low unemployment 43

Net New Jobs 43

Chapter 4 Clinton paved the way 47

Required Monthly Jobs Created 50

Job Creator Legacy 54

Unemployment 56

Average Unemployment Rate by President 60

Average Weeks Unemployed 61

Average Weeks of Unemployment by President 62

Total Americans employed 63

Number of Americans Unemployed 63

Chapter 5 Healthcare 66

Chapter 6 International disaster 76

Iran 82

Iraq 85

Israel 89

Afghanistan 90

Quick note about bin Laden 92

Drones killing women\children (is not a recruiting tool) 94

Chapter 7 Gasoline Prices 95

Chapter 8 National Debt 102

Chapter 9 Voting rights 104

Not One American Vote Diluted – Not One! 107

Marilyn Monroe and Babe Ruth voted in 2008 108

How Irresponsible Can You Be 111

Fix the Actual Problem 113

Chapter 10 Watergate II 115

Chapter 11 Leaks 121

Chapter 12 Race in Politics 124

Chapter 13 Media 130

Why Americans need to GET A CLUE! 130

Hypocrisy is rampant… 140

U.S. Credit Rating 143

End of the Book 146

Appendix 148

Food stamps 148

Figure 1 – Americans on Food Stamps and Costs by year 150

Figure 2 – Number on Food Stamps and Cost Details 152

Figure 3 – Chart of Growth in the Food Stamps Program 153

Unemployment and Employment 154

Figure 4 - Monthly Net New American Jobs 154

Figure 5 - Unemployment Rate 156

Figure 6 – Number Unemployed 158

Figure 9 – Average Weeks Unemployed 160

Figure 10 – Discouraged Workers 162

Figure 11 – Total Americans with Jobs 163

About the Author 166

The End 170

FORWARD

Most Americans cannot stand the boring, slow paced, archaic processes that define Washington, D.C. We are faced paced, multi-tasking creatures – so much so that we walk heads down looking at a smartphone, because walking alone is not stimulating enough. I am writing this book in a format that is easy to read, easy to understand, and easy to digest. One of the strongest criticisms I have of many pundits – is that they complicate things assuming everyone understands. Most do not have the background, points of reference, and pay little attention to Washington.

This book should help almost anyone to better understand what is being said (or not being said) to be able to make a truly educated decision when voting. Parents should give this book to their adult children who vote or will vote soon. Young Americans are very tech savvy, and will know in seconds when a politician is just saying what they want to hear in order to get their vote on Election Day!

I will not use titles throughout the book once someone is introduced. To repeat over and over that *President* Clinton, *President* Bush, or *Secretary of State* Colin Powell … over and over would be a waste of paper and your time. So please do not email me because I simply say Bush did this or Obama did that.

I will try to move quickly. I will present data from a number of sources – but the point of the book is to encourage skepticism. Bold statements are made and for some reason, if they line up with deep held beliefs or political persuasion, they are acceptable regardless… even if completely impossible!

I will provide examples that should show – in very simple terms - that it is a calculated activity intended to build a Legacy of Success. And if you pay close attention to specific wording, you will also pick up what I call the "double meaning" words. For example, I used to always tell a friend Terry that I "may" see him Friday after work for happy hour at a place called Wimbledon's in NY. I almost never actually intended to go – so I was careful to never say that I "will" see him at happy hour. On the other hand, the word "may" can and will have a completely different meaning when used as a response to a child who just asked to be excused from the dinner table. "Yes you may" will always be followed by the action – in this case leaving the dinner table. That is a simple example of a "double meaning" word. We will see much more sophisticated use of these types of words in Legacy Building.

But you will need to "man up" and face the facts. And by that I mean, you need to shake off the "deer in highlights" daze when you see a politician you are enamored with – especially when that politician is READING! He or She is reading BECAUSE they must get the wording precisely correct. One slight change to a word may cause the statement to be an outright lie. So, as you will see, great care is put into the choice of words and phrases. For example, do you see the difference between "a" and "b" below:

a. "Over 3000 Green Jobs resulted from the program"
b. "Over 3000 new Green Jobs resulted from the program"

You would not believe the incredible difference that the word "new" makes in the actual meaning of the statement! It changes everything! And the difference could be so huge when counting jobs. Plenty of jobs would qualify for statement "a". In fact, even those jobs that have been around for years or decades are easily reclassified as Green Jobs and would be included in the 3000 jobs described in statement "a". However, these same jobs would not be included in the 3000 "new" jobs described by statement "b".

And this is why you will never hear words like "new" or "net new" when ANYONE talks about Green Jobs! And do you think it is a little disingenuous to reclassify a job as Green Job if it has been around for decades – for example, should politicians really imply that a car pool parking attendant position that has been around for 15 years is now called a "Green Job"? And this is one of the so called "jobs created" when asked to justify spending taxpayer money? And isn't it deceptive to imply that this job is "...one of thousands of green jobs created...", when it was, in fact, created by reclassify the position; not by adding a net new job?

Imagine if I sold the public on believing that Kudzu (a plant that is taking over everywhere in Atlanta) was a valid replacement for gasoline, and convinced the public to spend $$ on the Kudzu industry. Imagine if I promised to use the funds to help create jobs in the kudzu industry, and then claimed thousands of jobs were created with the money. Would you be upset when you found out that the number of "jobs created" included every county worker who mows the lawns on every Atlanta highway? And that these "new jobs" were not new at all! Would that bother you? Well, incredibly, in Congressional testimony in June of 2012, the Obama Administration admitted that their "green jobs" number includes jobs that have been around for years and were just reclassified as "green jobs" to make the "green jobs" number look better. Keep in mind, if the U.S. created 10 jobs paying $100k a year, but had to spend $20 million to do so, it means the U.S. spent $2 million dollars per job. Contrast that to what Google, Apple or Microsoft "spend" for each job they add! Especially in lieu of the fact that so many of the companies that received billions of dollars in tax payer money for "green jobs" have already gone out of business.

If a sentence made about Green Jobs doesn't include the phrase "net new" then jobs may have actually been lost. You see without the phrase "net new", even if there were 3500 jobs in 2010 and only 3000 jobs in 2012 – the proper phase used in conjunction with "double meaning" words, and anyone can easily imply that thousands of brand new jobs were created – even if not one job was created. Test my theory. Turn up the TV next time you hear anyone talking about Green Jobs! You'll see…

Good Intentions – Disaster Results

Sometimes even the best, heartfelt intentions lead to the exact opposite result. This will most often happen when someone who's strong ego leads them to believe they can sum up and resolve any problem after a summary briefing – and then are given the power to actually act on this snap decision.

"We want to eliminate hunger in the world within 5 years." sounds like a noble cause. Who could find fault in that? But what happens if a plan is put in place that actually results in an increase in the number of hungry in the world at the end of 5 years? Then what? Do you just say, "oh well… our heart was in the right place?" If good intentions to eliminate the uninsured in America, results in an increase in uninsured, then what's the point? Just to say we tried?

There was a small village in Central America where many of the pathetically poor residents roamed the local dump for food. There was no "industry" to speak of anywhere within 20 miles. So when a U.S. based firm, working in conjunction with the leaders of the local government, opened a garment manufacturing facility, the residents were thrilled. They were happen to work rather than beg. The pay was low relative to western society, but was well above the region. For over a year, the company expanded the facility and the local people were pleased.

What could go wrong? Well, a group of college students in the U.S. heard about a small village in Central America where a U.S based firm was paying employees so low that some of the residents resorted to finding food in a local dump. They then decided that they should write letters to the company demanding higher wages, and then began to protest at the company headquarters.

After several months of protests and bad press, the company decided to close the plant and move the jobs to another location in Asia. Now all the residents are back to roaming the dump for food. When told of the full story and the results of their efforts actually caused more people to resort to the dump for food, the students were sad. "We didn't know", was all they could say. They seemed very sad. Then one suggested that they should go to Starbucks – and off they went, laughing and seemingly unaware of the consequences of what they had done…

Sometimes even the best intentions do have devastating results.

We all would like 100% of Americans to have medical insurance. But what good is it – if the care is substandard, rationed, and there are medication shortages. When you hear about shortages in prescription drugs recently – don't you realize what has caused this?

If you die while waiting for surgery, does it help to know that the healthy college student down the street now has medical insurance? And that student has insurance regardless of whether she/he will ever use the healthcare insurance or not. "I never get sick" is the number one reason young Americans decide not to purchase insurance. After high school and/or college, most young Americans do not earn much money. Paying a few hundred dollars a month for a policy is difficult when you are already paying a third or more of your paycheck to various taxes. Young Americans are not really the "free riders" that should be scrutinized. And it's a moot point since major healthcare insurance providers announced that they now cover young people on their parent's insurance policy – and will do so in the future even if the new healthcare law goes away.

The point is, seeing 100% of Americans with Health Insurance sounds really good. But if the reality is that 100% coverage means everyone must wait 6 months to see a doctor, then how is that good? Keep in mind that (on average over the last 50 years) more than 83% of Americans have Health Insurance. They like it and want to keep it. They like their doctor and want to keep that doctor. We have all heard of the horror stories where waiting 6 months for a doctor's appointment is common in countries with "socialized medical systems". If the U.S. moves in that direction, it may be even worse – some predict you will see one doctor (chosen by who knows) for EVERYTHING. Specialists will be available to the ultra-rich only - those who can simply pay for an awesome health policy or will pay "out of pocket" when care is needed. One doctor acts as your general physician, dentist, eye doctor, heart specialist … get my point comrade?

Words – Carefully chosen, carefully read!

We will explore some of the most outrageously misleading comments. For example, most would never believe the number of people involved, the amount of time required, and the legal review of one seemingly simple statement in a speech. "We excluded lobbyists from policymaking jobs." sounds like a straightforward statement. This is what Obama said in January 2010. No lobbyist were hired – might be the safe assumption of many who heard that statement. Well… not so fast. This one statement was crafted by several people, went through numerous revisions, and was reviewed by Legal, before Obama read it on January 27th 2010. It was crafted to cause the assumption that no lobbyists were hired… without having to blatantly lie. Hundreds of lobbyists were hired! Can you see how this could also be true? Can you see that this cleverly crafted statement actually does allow for this truth… also? See it now? Most would need to have this pointed out. Instead of saying, "No lobbyists were hired." the team formed a statement that sounds like that is exactly what they are saying. The use of the word "excluded" was chosen because it implies one meaning while allowing many meanings. And, of course, context is the key. If someone stated, "we *excluded* stepping on sea shells as we walked along the beach", I am sure that nobody would assume that someone could walk along the beach without stepping on any sea shells. One visualizes people walking in a zig-zag pattern, but still stepping on some shells. But, honestly, what did you assume when you first read the statement above about hiring lobbyists. Didn't you think that *none* were hired? And to double down on the ambiguity, what does "policymaking jobs" really mean? So add this to the end of the statement and wham - deception at its finest. This also explains the need for a teleprompter. Who is really going to be able to remember to say precisely what is crafted? Reading it - is a much safer approach. Weird, yet telling statements like, "… we've been to fifty-seven states" just would not have happened when reading. Obviously Obama was not reading the teleprompter when he said that back in 2008.

So, with that quick illustration of the level of effort going into building a legacy, I will layout in a clearly understood way, how facts will not deter a successful legacy for Obama.

Some will argue that I have no crystal ball – so what is the basis for my claim to see the future? It is based on observations along with feelings of deja vu. Claims are made, repeated over and over by supporters, and then reported by the press - without any fact checking. These "facts" appear in books, are included in made for TV movies, and these claims are so pounded into our heads – that even those of us who know for sure they are false, will even catch ourselves repeating the lie. This same thing happened during the Clinton Administration. So I will use a few examples from the 90s that will clearly show my theory to anyone who is interested in the actual truth. Even recently, claims were made about the 1990s that are absolutely false – statements that are the complete opposite of the truth. And this is important when examining sentences being made now. Legacy Building is in full force by the Obama team.

Let's play a game

To really highlight the vast discrepancies between facts and legacy, I want you to put this book down for 10 minutes. Jot down on a piece of paper the top five "legacy" bullet points you think of for each of the previous presidents. Depending on your age, you may not be able to go too far back. Do what you can – at least list legacy points for Bush and Clinton. If you can also put down a few points about Bush (senior) and Reagan that would be awesome! Later, we can review this list to see if it is consistent with the facts! You will be amazed! I will reference data from the BLS (Bureau of Labor Statistics), CBO (Congressional Budget Office), and other sources. This means you can verify anything quickly. I am not an insider, former Washingtonian, or renowned author. I simply like to research info – and was shocked to see the facts, based on the BS we hear regularly.

The Obama Legacy is going to be one of incredible successes.

It will include robust growth, balanced budgets, low unemployment, low gasoline prices, and a thriving real estate market driving the middle class. Oh, and he will claim credit for providing medical insurance for the 40 plus million Americans with no medical insurance, regardless if there are more than 50 million un-insured when he leaves office. Pesky facts…

Each chapter will discuss one area. I will use examples from previous Administrations to show how the process really can work – with consistent repeated claims; no matter how ridicules the statement seems … at the time. If you only have time to read a handful of chapters, then read the first half of the book and the final chapter (Media). The second half talks about specific areas – in an attempt to re-enforce what is covered in the 1st half of the book. And also, we will see how these keywords and phrases that are used to deceive you about jobs, the deficit and food stamps, are also used in other areas like Voters Rights and International Affairs.

For example, in 2010, we heard for the first time ever in this great country's history, a metric that was designed ENTIRELY to deceive you! Remember hearing the phrase "Created or Saved" millions of jobs? When you are losing a million jobs a year, like this country was, you get very creative to avoid answering truthfully about failures….

As another quick example, Bush's Legacy includes the Bush "tax cuts for the rich". It's something repeated by the media over and over and over…… Yet, everyone knows that 70% of that tax cut bill is for the Middle Class. Less than 1/3 of the cuts go to rich, and the majority of those go to small businesses. How do we know that? Because both the Democrats and Republicans tell us that 70% of the impact is on the middle class each year when the cuts are going to expire. They tell us that if they don't extend the tax cuts – it will result in a huge tax increase on the middle class. Both Republicans and Democrats have submitted bills that will fix the loopholes that allow a few large companies to bay low tax rates – but they never vote on the bills. And both parties have reasons to maintain the stalemate. But that is a topic for another book.

Steps to building a Legacy

- ✓ Decide on legacy highlights
- ✓ Schedule dates for announcements that form the legacy points
- ✓ Have legal review critical statements
- ✓ Say "odd" things during speeches, regardless of facts known
- ✓ Avoid all follow up questions
- ✓ Collusion with the press is required (i.e. Bush's Mission Accomplished - example where the press didn't cooperate)
- ✓ Repetition is important – so insert the phrase everywhere
- ✓ Write memoirs and/or books including "odd" statements
- ✓ Encourage proponents to reference false claims while on TV and/or in books they write

"I was the top Salesperson at a multinational firm for 6 years in a row!"

That sounds really impressive… until you find out that there was only one salesperson at the firm for all those years. Declining to answer questions after a speech insulates the accurate and complete truth. The question, "How many sales people were there?" would quickly clear up the ambiguity.

"Remember me? I am the guy who gave you surpluses for four years", said Bill Clinton.

Hmmmm…

CHAPTER 1

IT MAY SOUND "ODD"

"Look, the private sector is doing fine", was the way he phrased it, at the end of a discussion about U.S. jobs. It was that phrase that caused the room to become quiet. Surely he plans to announce some new data points that would back up that claim. Was there a major correction to the much studied Jobs Report? Did an error somewhere cause a revision to the well-known and gloomy unemployment numbers? But as the press pool waited, Obama went on to talk about another topic.

But wait! What was that he just said about the private sector? Doing fine? Did he just misspeak? Maybe he said "not doing fine" and we just couldn't hear the word "not". Reporters looked at each other, as if it was just announced that all cars in the press pool parking area had been towed.

That statement was…. well it was just plain odd!

Certain presidents seem to understand that building a legacy is hard work. You often need to say things that, at the time, seem very odd. For example, if your plan is to say that as president you turned a near depression into a growing economy (and the actual facts say otherwise), then you may need to make statements that seem to contradict the truth. But if you carefully select your wording, no one will even realize what you are actually doing. This allows the president to take that snippet – and use it to build the foundation of a legacy around any issues he/she chooses!

I predict that by 2020, we will all hear how it took Obama less than three years to create a growing, thriving economy – with low unemployment, low gas prices, balanced budgets, and medical care for all Americans. We will hear that Obama ended all the wars, and everyone in the world loves America because of his efforts. Ignoring the reports that the number of homes in foreclosure is at the highest point in decades, the number of recipients receiving food-stamps hit all-time highs in 2012, and un-employment is higher and averaging twice the length in duration (40 weeks as opposed to averaging 20 weeks since the 70s). Gas prices have come down from highs – but is anyone happy still paying more than $3 a gallon (almost double the price when Obama entered office). The number of Americans without health insurance has exploded since 2010 - after being fundamentally stagnate at 15% (give or take 3%) for the last few decades. Obama's legacy will require a substantial rewrite of the facts. And collusion with news services is critical. If Obama says that cars can be powered by pollen or bee larvae, it's critical that no one question the claim. (Ever notice that after most speeches are complete, no questions are taken.)

Not convinced?

"Since I've been president, federal spending has risen at the lowest rate in nearly 60 years."

Incredibly, this is what Obama said in a speech he gave in June 2012. What? In what universe could this statement be true? As you can see below, this is false. He then went on to say republicans bamboozled Americans – that republicans "run up these wild debts and then when we take over, we have to clean it up". (Watch how very carefully Obama reads the teleprompter when he makes the claim "lowest rate in nearly 60 years".)

Facts show that the opposite is true! The unbelievable leap in the U.S. nation debt is a direct result of the dramatic increase in federal spending under Obama!

FACT: It took 16 years for Clinton and Bush to add $6 trillion to the national debt. In only 4 years Obama added $6 trillion!

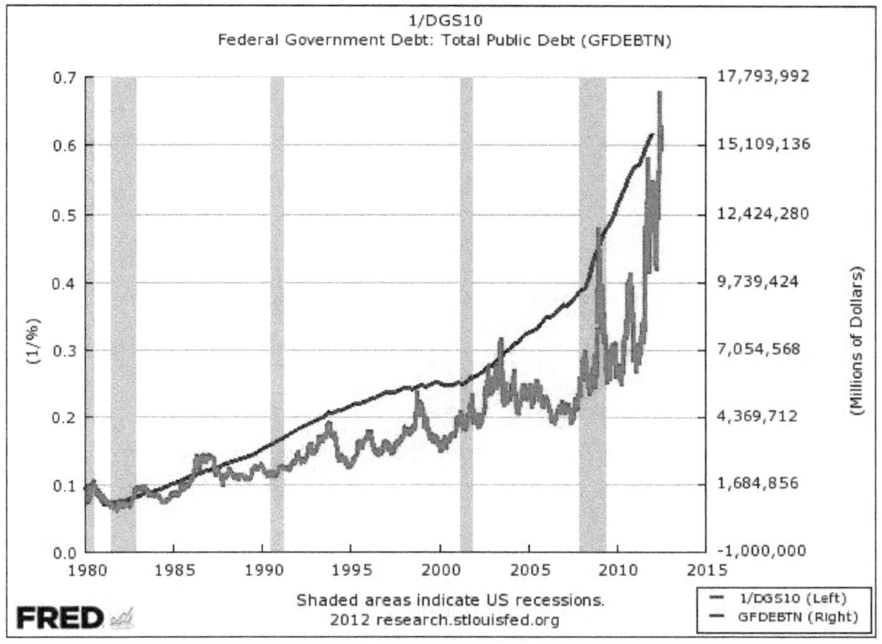

Even some his biggest supporters wondered how in the world Obama planned to explain this obvious false assertion. Most assumed someone from the many news organizations attending the press conference would question that claim. No? Yet, no one did. Even the most junior reporters are aware that Obama has dramatically increased spending, and has driven up the U.S debt. In fact, spending has increased under Obama, by any and all metrics, faster than ever before. And it's reflected in the explosive growth of the national debt. Clinton and Bush each added trillions to the national – about $6 trillion combined - but it took 16 years to add that amount.

Obama has increased the debt by over $5.9 trillion in less than 4 years!

Eventually, someone in the Obama Administration produced documents to try to explain this ridicules assertion. Needless to say, the clarification was even more ridicules. I won't break it down here – suffice it to say that they basically left out many spending programs from their formula. No one is sure how anyone could think that is even remotely logical, since all of the money was spent years after Obama took office. (In fact, Reagan had 8 balanced budgets – if you leave out spending programs from the Carter years. Bush had surpluses! Give me a break!)

No reporters challenged the clarification…

It is so obvious why the problem can never be solved – when viewed from a "project management" standpoint. The problem is – that nothing in Washington can be viewed logically. There is always a "political lens" clouding the problem.

Chuck is leading a project to move diamonds from deep in the forest to a roadway that can support trucks. Bob is Chuck's assistant and he has a team of 20 men and 50 donkeys. Since the diamonds are plentiful in this extremely remote section of the jungle, there is always a huge pile of diamonds waiting for the donkeys to make the round trip and return for another load. But Chuck is so confused by the small amount of diamonds making the difficult donkey based journey. So he sends another 50 donkeys. But even with the additional 50 donkeys, there is no increase in diamonds. So Cuck decides to take the journey deep into the jungle to see what is happening. Bob greets Chuck and proudly shows off the work he is leading. "And look at that pile of diamonds! It's much higher than ever before! We may need to start a second pile." But Chuck was wondering where all the donkeys he had sent over were? With all those diamonds waiting, there should be a steady stream of donkeys carry the diamonds through the jungle. Chuck does see an occasional donkey, slowly trudge in or out of the jungle – but only a few and they all looked exhausted! "Where are the donkeys Bill? I sent over another 50 but I don't see them and the production has not increased at all". Bill points toward a valley just beyond a small hill. Bill and Chuck walk up the hill and looking out over the valley they see an open field with donkeys everywhere! The donkeys are actually in one of two groups:

- *50 donkeys in a pasture*
- *35 donkeys under a huge shade tree*

Chuck asks Bill why the donkeys are in the valley rather than moving diamonds. "Don't you see why the diamonds are piling up?" Chuck asked Bill while pointing to the pile of diamonds and starting to show his impatience… Bill sits Chuck down and explains that the diamonds are being moved – but mostly by 15 donkeys – which explained the exhausted donkeys Chuck did see working. He went on to say that the 15 strongest donkeys were doing 80% of the work. And the 35 medium size donkeys resting under the shade tree, did the other 20% of the work.

But Chuck wanted to know about the other 50 donkeys – the ones in the valley? Bill explained that those were smaller donkeys and he they did not assist at all. Chuck patiently told Bill that he now understood what the problem was to cause the diamonds to pile up.

With half the donkeys doing no work and another one third of the donkeys only helping a little bit – the pile of diamonds continued to increase? And also, that the 15 donkeys (doing all the work) were about to keel over. They were being overworked and couldn't be expected to do all the work.

Chuck pointed out that Bill should have used the 50 smaller donkeys and had them carry smaller bundles of diamonds – rather than nothing at all. The 15 stronger donkeys would never be able to reduce the pile regardless of how much they carried! Chuck pointed out the flaw in Bill's system. Chuck set up a new system. The strong donkeys each carried 50 diamonds and the smaller and medium donkeys carry 30 diamonds each, then:

85 donkeys carry 30 = 2550
15 donkeys carry 50 = 750
Total per trip = 3300

So did Bill see his error? Did he see how the pile would decrease ONLY if he relied on all the donkeys? No – and Bill was fired!

This is how our government incorrectly applies the progressive tax system. And also why the U.S. (logically) will never eliminate the debt.

To be perfectly clear - most of the deficit problem is overspending. However on the revenue side, the problem is not understood by politicians, so they are always looking for the solution in the wrong place. They focus on the exhausted 15 donkeys, when the real answer is to ask those that pay nothing - to pay a tiny bit. But the tax system has been bastardized over the years so that approximately half Americans pay no federal taxes – none, zero, nada, zilch! And the huge companies like GE pay accountants millions of dollars to avoid paying federal taxes – and have moved millions of jobs overseas to avoid the high U.S. Corporate taxes. This leaves a small group of middle class paying more than they can afford – to make up for the 50% that pay nothing – but this approach will never reduce the debt! Almost every country in the civilized world has reduced corporate tax rates to encourage companies to move there – the U.S. has not kept up with the rest of the world and now has the highest Corporate Tax Rate! So raising Corporate rates sounds good, but the result is massive layoffs of Americans.

Listen, neither Republicans nor Democrats want to end the corporate tax loopholes! The common misconception is that only Republicans protect Corporations. Nonsense! Nothing could be further from the truth! Democrats had 2 years (2008-2010) to change the tax code to end corporate loopholes. They passed practically any bill they wanted, and the super majority the Democrats had at the time kept Republicans silent. And yet, the Democrats did not fix the loopholes! Anyone in the media ask them why not? Of course not!

Remember – Obama plans to have a legacy of balanced budgets. The only debate is whether he accomplished a balanced budget after only one year in office, or if it took 18-24 months. The "odd" statement about spending at a lower rate in 60 years is the 1st clue.

Facts will not get in the way.

CHAPTER 2

TRICKS, GIMMICKS, AND REPETITION

The key is to constantly repeat the statement that builds the legacy you desire.

You may have also noticed, in the chart above, that the national debt has risen for every president for the 32 years shown. Look at the years 1993 – 2001. The debt rose trillions of dollars under the Clinton Administration, despite the odd assertion by some of annual "surpluses".

My son came to me one day and expressed concern that he and his family were spending more than they earned. I told him to set up a reasonable budget – and the problem would solve itself. In June, he emailed saying they reversed the trend of overspending and actually saved money in May. He said they planned to save money every month going forward. One year later I asked him how he was doing with the budget. He sighed. He went on to say that during the months of May and June, they stuck to their budget and had actually spent less that they took in. I said, "ah… a surplus. Surpluses are good." He nodded then showed me a document that detailed the last twelve months. Unfortunately, the document showed that they spent much more than they earned every month – except the two months of May and June. In fact, in September alone they spent 4x the "surplus" from May and June. So they never actually put a dime in the bank. Instead of ending the year reducing their debt, they owed much more than they did twelve months earlier. To make matters worse, my son said that he bragged to friends and family back in June about eliminating his debt by sticking to a strict budget….

This is what Clinton did.

Let's explore the similarities between what Obama is doing now, with what Clinton did then. We will also see how well it worked, and see how it's key to Legacy Building.

Many of us were wondering if Clinton was still inhaling when he stood in front of a chart showing that he had balanced the budget. The Chart looked like someone had drawn a huge, upside down letter "U" on a poster size piece of paper – indicating a reversal of sky rocketing debt to budget surplus. Clinton told the crowd that not only had he balanced the budget, but that there were huge surpluses forecast for many years! This sounded awesome. Could it be true?

But wait, the CBO's most recent report predicted annual deficits for years to come. And Democrats were using this report, just weeks before, to demand higher taxes.

The Clinton Team submitted a 10 Year Plan based on fantasy…

So how is it, that Clinton was now saying this? Economists were mystified. The news reporters seemed confused … but remained quiet. Even though most thought this must be the result of trickery and gimmicks, no one challenged the assertion.

(Could this be Legacy Building in motion? Is this a clue?)

What the Clinton Administration DID DO, was submitt a 10 year plan based on fantasy. It projected such a rosy picture of the next 10 years, that many thought it was a joke! And when it was clear that it wasn't a joke, and Clinton was serious, people just shrugged and wondered what he was up to? It projected extremely low unemployment. Like unprecedentedly low unemployment for a prolong period that the U.S. has never seen. And, assuming "full employment" (defined as 4% or lower) for several years, payments made to those on welfare, food stamps, school lunches and others would be slashed. In fact, those now receiving payments for social services like welfare, unemployment, and food stamps, would be employed and paying taxes – as a result of "full employment". And if that wasn't enough fantasy for you, the 10 Year Plan assumed billions in savings of waste and fraud, yet included no details about how that would be accomplished. It assumed unrealistically low interest on the outstanding debt. THIS IS BIG SINCE .40 CENTS OF EVERY DOLLAR SPENT IS TO PAY INTEREST ON THE DEBT! And it goes on and on … reductions in military expenditures that not one sane person would imagine happening. Reductions in aid overseas… wars and illness globally decreasing or disappearing… oh, he inhaled! You better believe he inhaled!

So, when you examine the REALITY (sorry to be a buzz kill Bill), none of these "projections" were even close! In fact, the economy drifted into recession the last year Clinton was in office which resulted in a huge increase in payments (food stamps and welfare), unemployment skyrocketed and those people stopped paying any taxes on wages. The poor increased – so they continued to get payments, and certainly didn't pay taxes due to their new career! The savings due to reductions in fraud and waste never happened, the U.S. increased aid overseas, and illnesses like AIDS increased along with U.S. funding. And one thing the Clinton team never wants to talk about. The costs associated with the attacks of 9/11 were not included in his "rosy forecast" – Not one dime! Had the Clinton Administration been more diligent during the 1990s – instead of virtually MIA, we could have killed bin Laden and al Qaeda leaders. The September 11th attacks were planned for years while Clinton was at the helm. They were postponed several times – so saying it happened when Bush was in office is nonsense! And the aftermath of September 11th added trillions to the budgets. And guess what, the rosy 10 Year Plan submitted by Clinton didn't include any of those costs.

The point is – rather than deal with terrorism attacks "on the cheap", maybe we could have stopped the attacks of 9/11? Maybe if we spent just a little money and went on the offense against al Qaeda, we wouldn't have seen nearly 3000 American civilians slaughtered.

That is what I wonder when I hear the "surplus lie" repeated!

Fifteen years later, Clinton now claims he had "four balanced budgets". And no one challenges that ridicules assertion! Anyone with a computer and internet access can research the national debt during Clinton's years to find out the truth. And not spending money on U.S. security prior to the attacks of September 11 2001 is certainly something I would not brag about!

Shall we start with the basics? Then we can dive into the details to show how any Legacy can be the exact opposite of the truth.

Clinton years in office (Jan 20th 1993 thru Jan 20th 2001):

At the end of 1992, the national debt: $4.0 trillion

At the end of 2000, the national debt: $5.62 trillion

So Clinton actually raised the debt more than any other president before him, except Ronald Reagan, then went on to claim "balance budgets" and "surpluses as far as the eye can see". Sweet!

Let's dive in deeper. Here is actual data broken down by year. I see no reduction in debt – do you? Certainly from a year to year basis, THERE IS NO SURPLUS – NOT EVEN ONE YEAR! As you can see, each year the national debt increased. (Just as the son, in the story above, who saved money during 2 months, but overspent during the other 10 months – the results are the same. In both cases, isn't it rather disingenuous to talk about surpluses?)

Do you see how it does happen - even when the facts clearly show the reality - the facts will not prevent a Legacy if the president is persistent, and there is collusion with the U.S. press?

Year	U.S. Debt – ($billion)
1990	3206.29
1991	3598.18
1992	4001.79
1993	4351.04
1994	4643.31
1995	4920.58
1996	5181.46
1997	5369.21
1998	5478.19
1999	5605.52
2000	5628.70
2001	5769.89
2002	6198.40
2003	6760.02
2004	7354.65
2005	7905.30
2006	8451.35
2007	8950.75
2008	9986.08
2009	11875.85
2010	13528.81
2011	14764.23
2012	16350.88 (projected)
2013	17547.90 (projected)

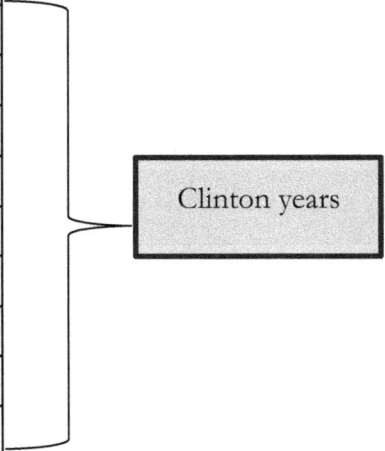

Clinton years

By the way, it took me approximately 4 minutes to search, retrieve and verify the data above. So when you now hear Clinton make these baseless claims, keep in mind that the wording of the statement is no coincidence. And all the press - every reporter and every news anchor is fully aware of the truth. It's like when grandpa says he leaving in the morning to go stop the Nazis, and family members just smile and say nothing.

Former Clinton team members and supporters proudly claim that they submitted a "10 year forecast" showing surpluses, and eventually eliminating the debt. Oh brother!

Now with your newly honed skillset at dissecting a statement, you now know this is meaningless!

1. Is sure is easy to project a rosy future in 10 years! Especially when you will have been out of office for eight of those years.
2. "Forecast" is a clever little word. Imagine if I told my wife that I was forecasting doubling my income, reducing costs, and putting more money into savings. Then I showed her the budget. Then I handed off the budget responsibility to her. I did increase my income, but only by 50%. Earning more income meant I needed nicer clothing, and a newer car. Gasoline and food prices went up (not in my forecast) and we didn't save additional money. Can I really say I "handed" her surpluses and she turned them into deficits? *Come on – let's get real!*

3. The forecast made assumptions around growth that were so high as to be unprecedented in U.S. history. Inflation was projected to stay low. No one predicted a Homeland Security department. The forecast didn't include any money to defend America and destroy those who attacked us (in one of the so called "unfunded wars"). And while many complained about the "slow Federal response" to Katrina (when in fact the response was delayed entirely by local and state leaders), that storm also added billions to the budget.

So, it is really *very* naive to think there is any truth to statements by Clinton (who earned the nickname of Slick Willy) that he had surpluses while in office and/or he left the U.S. economy with a balanced budget. It's simply not backed up by the easily verifiable numbers.

In fact, the national debt increased every year Clinton was in office. So if there was a surplus, he and Gore must have pocketed it. "There was a surplus, but the debt increased due to interest", was how one Clinton advisor *tried* to explain the increase in debt each year under Clinton. Nonsense! Interest payments on the debt are included as a line item. But the reporter did not challenge him. This is a Legacy Building requirement. "Remember me? I am the guy who gave you 4 years of surpluses…." is what Clinton says now.

Look, I am not picking on Clinton. No president has actually had a surplus since the depression. It's just that he is the first to try to make that claim. This book is about Legacy Building. This is a great example of the "off the wall" statements that MUST be made, if the legacy is to stick. Especially if the legacy you want is the exact opposite of the facts.

Double Meanings Words

This is a simple concept. There are ways to use certain words or phrases that sound like you are saying one thing when you are in fact saying the exact opposite. Check this out – the way a huge tax increase was announced was to describe it as a tax that only affected 3% of companies.

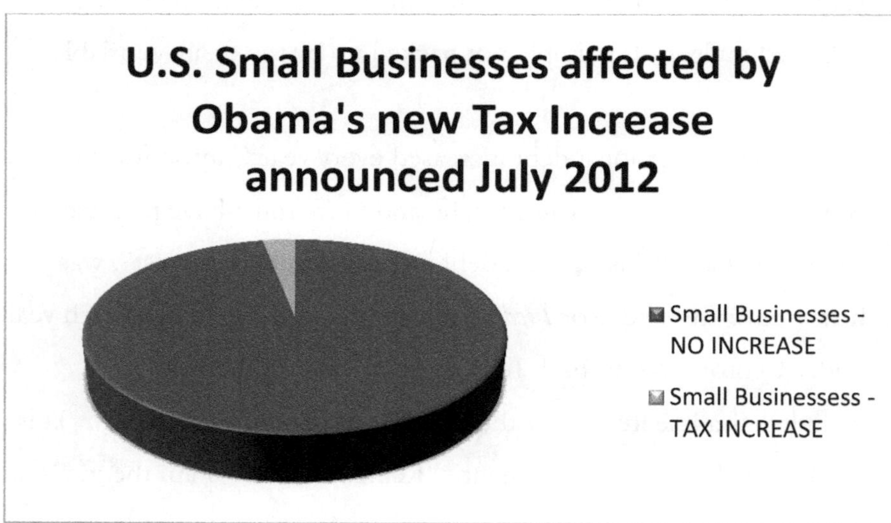

With only that data, most would say that while we should not raise taxes for any small businesses, 3% is a small amount and shouldn't impact much. I mean, how many American jobs could be affected by this tax increase? It must be a tiny amount … right?

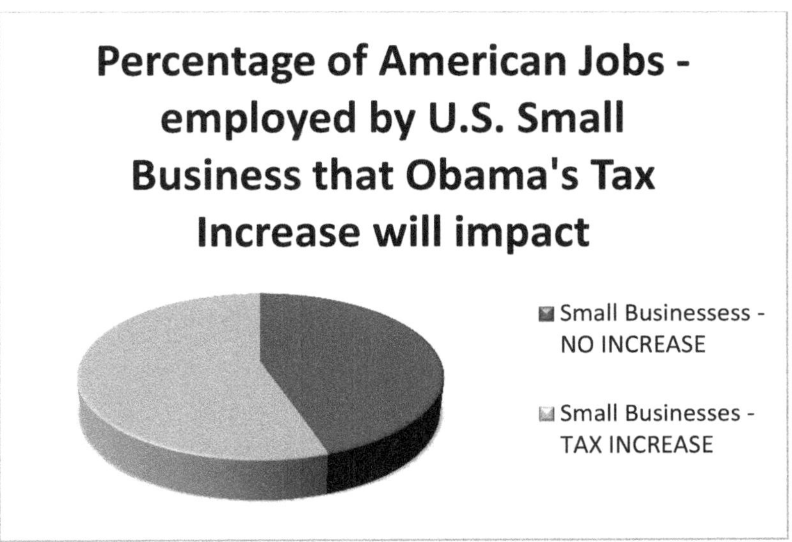

So even when the wording seems perfectly clear, proper use of "double meaning" words allows a clever individual to imply, or encourage a very different understanding. No worries – you just need to ask follow up questions. Questions like, "of the Americans employed by Small Businesses, how many of those Americans work for a small businesses that will see taxes increase?" is the question that must be asked. It was not! ANSWER - 55%

By preventing follow up questions, one can easily create the wrong understanding of the facts while not actually lying. But does anyone think the wording wasn't chosen to deceive? Later, we will see how media collusion is critical to make sure that appropriate follow up question is never asked!

Legacy Building is hard work and requires significant planning and execution. And it has to be at least remotely possible.

Obviously, there are failures: "I took the initiative - creating the Internet" said Al Gore in the late 1990s.

This one didn't take.

CHAPTER 3

LEGACY OF LOW UNEMPLOYMENT

Obama says over and over, "… we created over 4 million jobs…"

Hmmmm… But he is forgetting about all the jobs lost? Using that formula, Bush created 24 million jobs, and Clinton created even more. Even Carter could say he created jobs using that approach. *Come on now. We said we were getting real.*

Net New Jobs

As additional people come in to the workforce (as the population grows due to births and legal migration), the economy must create jobs, just to keep up with population growth. To be fair, the recession started at the end of the Bush Administration. However, the data shows that it actually became much worse once Obama's policies kicked in. As of this writing, Obama has a Net New Jobs of zero. Technically it's actually negative 500k. Net New Jobs – the true measurement of the job market.

Also, the U.S. workforce size is way down from its peak. During the boom years of 2006 and 2007 when unemployment hovered around 4.5% - many seniors and "stay home moms" entered the workforce. As we will see, they left the workforce in 2010 and have not returned.

The Bureau of Labor Statistics (BLS) shows that the Number of Working Americans has decreased under Obama to 134 million from a high of 146.5 million under Bush. Examine the chart below which shows the number of Americans working each year (million).

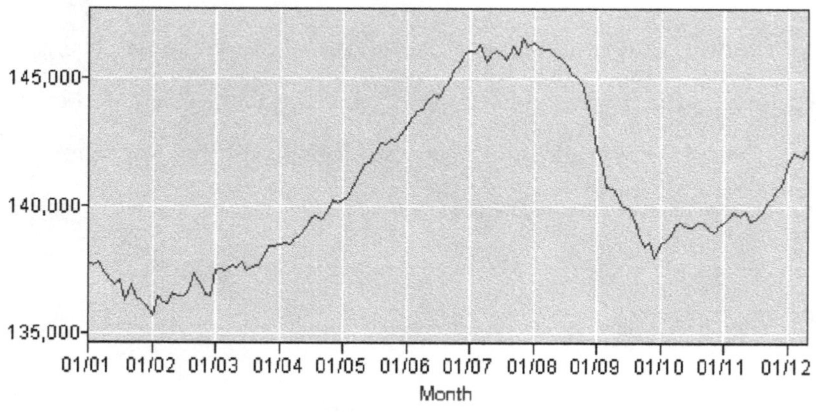

As you can clearly see, the number of American's working today, is much lower than the all-time high of 146.5 million reached in November 2007. Since Obama took over:

143,328,000 Americans working Dec 2008 (end of the Bush term)
141,865,000 Americans working as of April 2012
1,463,000 ***fewer*** Americans working

Here is the data (thousands):

Year	Jan	Feb	Mar	Apr	May	Jun	Jul	Aug	Sep	Oct	Nov	Dec
2001	137778	137612	137783	137299	137092	136873	137071	136241	136846	136392	136238	136047
2002	135701	136438	136177	136126	136539	136415	136413	136705	137302	137008	136521	136426
2003	137417	137482	137434	137633	137544	137790	137474	137549	137609	137984	138424	138411
2004	138472	138542	138453	138680	138852	139174	139556	139573	139487	139732	140231	140125
2005	140245	140385	140654	141254	141609	141714	142026	142434	142401	142548	142499	142752
2006	143150	143457	143741	143761	144089	144353	144202	144625	144815	145314	145534	145970
2007	146028	146057	146320	145586	145903	146063	145905	145682	146244	145946	146595	146273
2008	146397	146157	146108	146130	145929	145738	145530	145196	145059	144792	144078	143328
2009	142187	141660	140754	140654	140294	140003	139891	139458	138775	138401	138607	137968
2010	138500	138665	138836	139306	139340	139137	139139	139338	139344	139072	138937	139220
2011	139330	139551	139764	139628	139808	139385	139450	139754	140107	140297	140614	140790
2012	141637	142065	142034	141865								

Interesting observations:

- 137,778,000 Americans working Jan 2001
- 143,328,000 Americans working at the end of Dec 2008.

- Bush a net gain of 5.5 million Americans working after 8 years!
- So far, Obama has a net loss of 1,463,000 over 3.5 years

Quick note here – deceptive democrats will try to point out that Clinton, in comparison to Bush, created almost 4 times the number of jobs over 8 years. As we will see next:

- Bush Sr. left a roaring economy for Clinton that was pumping out an average of 240,000 jobs per month the 1st year!
    - First 12 months after Bush Sr., the U.S. had a net gain of 2.7 million jobs
    - First 21 months after Bush Sr., the U.S. had a net gain of 5.7 million jobs
- Clinton left a disaster! Clinton Recession was in effect when Bush Jr. took office –
    - First 12 months after Clinton, the U.S. had a net loss of 1.7 million jobs.
    - **First 21 months after Clinton, the U.S. had a net loss of 2.2 million jobs lost**

So using the facts above, now Americans know exactly why the early Clinton years were so good. Honestly, it's the mess Clinton left behind, that Americans criticize. And the ridicules claims about what he left behind is what we refuse to be silent about … any longer.

CHAPTER 4

CLINTON PAVED THE WAY

Learn from the king of deception….

How many times have you heard Clinton say he inherited a recession and left a growing economy? Is that accurate? Isn't the opposite actually the truth? Let's look at the number of jobs the U.S. economy was creating when Clinton became president versus when he left office. Based on the Clinton Legacy here, one would assume that when Clinton was sworn in Jan 20th 1993, the economy was losing jobs. And, when Clinton left office on Jan 20th 2001 – surely the U.S must have been creating 300k – 400k jobs every month?

Correct?

(Rule #1 – you cannot change the Legacy Points list you created earlier, after reading the section below.)

Look at the number of jobs created (below) each month in 2001 – and remember Clinton left office on Jan 20th, 2001.

So how is it that only one month, in the entire 2001 year, had POSITVE job growth? That was in February 2001, and it was a whopping 63k nationwide. Even more shocking is the fact that in only two months – ***of the first 21 months after Clinton left office*** - had positive job growth! So totaling the aforementioned 63k jobs February 2001, plus another 47k jobs in June 2002; the Bureau of Labor Statistics shows a total of 110k jobs were created in the immediate 21 months after Clinton left office. However, in those same 21 months however, the U.S. lost 2,382,200 jobs! This means the economy lost over 2.38 million jobs after Clinton left office!

Not exactly the way it was reported – or the way it's being reported today! Can you now see how the Legacy can completely contradict the facts? Below are the jobs created per month in the U.S. AFTER Clinton left office. (Bush was sworn in Jan 20th 2001):

Year	Jan	Feb	Mar	Apr	May	Jun	Jul	Aug	Sep	Oct	Nov	Dec
2001	-15	63	-28	-282	-44	-128	-125	-155	-243	-331	-295	-178
2002	-129	-146	-24	-84	-9	47	-100	-11	-55	121	8	-163
2003	95	-159	-213	-49	-9	0	25	-45	109	197	14	119

In fact:

- The U.S economy lost 1,762,000 jobs in 2001.
- The U.S economy lost almost 1 million jobs BEFORE 9/11.
- The U.S. created jobs in only one month in 2001 (February).
- In the 1st 21 months AFTER Clinton left office, only 2 months had positive job growth.
- The U.S. lost more jobs the 9 months BEFORE 9/11 - than were lost the 9 months AFTER 9/11.
- The U.S. had THE EXACT SAME number of months with positive job growth in the 9 months AFTER 9/11 as there were in the 9 months BRFORE 9/11 (one month)
- As we will see, in contrast, every month in 2004 had positive job creation.

And if that's not enough, **look at how awesome the economy was doing when Bill Clinton entered office.** George Bush senior handed over the keys to the White House to Bill Clinton on Jan 20th 1993. The Clinton Legacy never mentions how much better the economy was doing when he entered office (versus the mess it was when Clinton left office!) In fact, the recession from 1991 was shallow and really had ended before the November 1992 election. As the numbers show below, the U.S. economy was firing on all cylinders and pumping out jobs the day Clinton became president:

Year	Jan	Feb	Mar	Apr	May	Jun	Jul	Aug	Sep	Oct	Nov	Dec
1993	310	242	-51	308	265	174	295	160	239	278	261	307
1994	270	201	462	353	333	313	364	298	355	208	422	272

WOW! With the exception of March 1993, Bill Clinton inherited a robust and growing economy – with phenomenal job growth that we have not seen since. In truth, he left office with an economy in recession, losing jobs month after month, with skyrocketing deficits predicted until 2024.

Funny how some people like to re-write history. Legacy building is hard work. Clinton left a disaster. Why Republicans don't challenge any assertion contrary to the well documented facts is just amazing to me? And it's so easy to cite the data: http://data.bls.gov/timeseries/CES0000000001?output_view=net_1mth.

Required Monthly Jobs Created

Required Monthly Jobs Created is an interesting metric. It is the number of monthly jobs required to keep up with population growth. This number seems to vary, depending on who is president. Based on news reports and other "claims" from those who should know, here are the monthly numbers required per president:

Jimmy Carter – 200k	Bill Clinton – 175k
Ronald Reagan – 475k	George Bush Jr. - 300k
George Bush Sr. – 350k	Barack Obama – 125k

Anything less than the number defined is considered a failure. Who assigns these numbers? How is it fair? I don't have those answers.

By the way, once the Clinton recession ended, the country shook off the devastation of 9/11, and the Bush policies kicked in; the economy was doing very well in late 2003. By 2004, it was roaring, with exceptionally low unemployment… and did so until the November 2006 elections. Compare the job creation in 2004-2006 (below) vs. 2001-2003 job losses! Bush was never given credit for this huge turnaround!

From September 2003 thru June 2007, the U.S. economy had 37 months of consecutive job growth – except October 2006. During those 37 months, 7.867 million jobs were created minus the 9k lost in October 2006 – for a Net New Jobs total of 7.858 million jobs.

Hello!

Year	Jan	Feb	Mar	Apr	May	Jun	Jul	Aug	Sep	Oct	Nov	Dec
2004	162	44	337	249	310	81	46	122	161	348	63	134
2005	137	240	141	360	170	243	374	193	66	80	334	160
2006	283	316	283	181	14	76	209	183	157	-9	204	171

In fact, the 36 months for the years 2004 - 2006:

- The U.S had 15 months with 200k or more jobs created
- The U.S had 7 months with 300k or more jobs created
- The U.S had only 9 months with less than 100k jobs created
    - The U.S. had a gain of –
        - Over 2.0 million net new jobs in 2004
        - Over 2.4 million net new jobs in 2005
        - Over 2.0 million net new jobs in 2006
        - Over 1.1 million net new jobs in 2007

In fact, in the 5 years from January 2003 to December 2007, the U.S. pumped out a net gain of over 7.8 million jobs! (Remember from our earlier discussion, in 3.5 years, Obama has a net loss of about 500k.)

So what happened? What changed? The newly elected Democrats gained control of Congress in January 2007. Their policies started taking their toll on job creation shortly thereafter. And the results are clear - After having a net gain of 1.1 million jobs in 2007, the U. S. had a 3.6 million net loss of jobs in 2008.

Year	Jan	Feb	Mar	Apr	May	Jun	Jul	Aug	Sep	Oct	Nov	Dec
2007	236	93	190	72	139	75	-40	-18	73	79	112	89
2008	41	-84	-95	-208	-190	-198	-210	-274	-432	-489	-803	-661

In April 2008, when unemployment was 5.0%, who would ever believe 4 years later, we'd hear the media try to say that unemployment increasing from 8.1% to 8.2% is a good thing? Or that we'd hear the current administration trying to blame the previous administration for anything after being in office for nearly 4 years? What would the headline be if Bush blamed Clinton for anything in say, July 2004 after 3 ½ years running the show? The media would have pounced on Bush if he try to claim (in 2004) that he had actually balanced budgets 4 years in a row since he wasn't including money spent on anything he considered "Clinton programs". Bush could exclude money the Federal Government spent on social programs, defense spending, and even the war in Afghanistan since this was Clinton's mess due to his repeated refusal to take out bin Laden in the middle 1990s!

In 2012, It's awfully funny listening to people attempt to juggle the "blame". I heard Carney (WH Spokesman) try to take credit for 3 months of fair job growth, while blaming Bush for the weak job growth before and after the 3 months of fair job growth:

Jan 2009 to Nov 2011 – poor job growth all Bush's fault
Dec 2011 to Feb 2012 – fair job growth due to Obama's policies
Mar 2012 –to May 2012 – poor job growth all Bush's fault

Hysterical!

Job Creator Legacy

With the help of the left leaning press, repeating two phrases over and over … then combining the two … legacy is born. For example:

1. "… losing almost 800k jobs per month when I came into office…"
2. "… 27 months of consecutive job growth…"

With our new "parsing skill-set" we now know that 27 consecutive months of job growth is **terrible** - if each month we averaged less than 200k jobs per month. This claim is meaningless for several reasons:

1. It's 20 months - net loss of 27k jobs in September 2010
2. During the 20 months of job growth, the monthly job growth was lame –
    a. 100k jobs or less – 7 months
    b. Between 100k and 160k jobs – 6 months
    c. U.S. needs at least 250k jobs monthly to break even

Even if we had 10 years of consecutive job growth – of only 100 jobs per month… we would be in the worst depression ever!

Carter had a similar run of "consecutive months" of job growth for over 2 years. The job growth included months where we had huge monthly increases of more than 300k jobs –

- Oct 78 – 363k jobs
- Nov 78 – 437k jobs
- Mar 79 – 426k jobs
- May 79 – 372k jobs
- June 79 - 318k jobs

And we all know where we were just a few months later. Within a few months the economy collapsed!

And the statement about "800k jobs" is deceptive to say the least. We peaked out at a monthly loss of 818k jobs – that is true. But this statement implies that "losing 800k jobs a month" was the norm. And it makes the listener believe that the U.S. was losing 800k a month – month after month after month.

Would it shock you to know that there were only 2 months total that had job loses above 800k?

What's that you say? No one could be that calculated! No one could be that deceptive! Do the research – it will take you 3 minutes!

Unemployment

In 8 years, the Bush Administration registered only two months with unemployment above 6.5%. In nearly four years, Obama has had only one month of unemployment below 8%. And it shouldn't surprise anyone that the only month below 8% was his 1st month in office – January 2009.

The chart below will not be shown on TV in 2012. The U.S. press is primarily democrats – and it appears most have agreed to ONLY show unemployment charts from 2010 thru 2012. Without the previous years, one cannot see how outrageously high, and abnormal it is for the U.S. unemployment rate to be above 8%. You can also see that most recession are short – both the Bush recession of 1991 and the Clinton recession of 2000 ended quickly and was followed by strong monthly job growth ranging from 300k to 800k net new jobs.

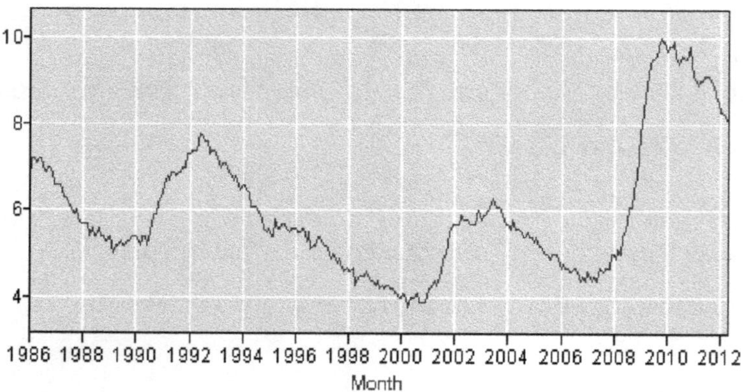

Examining the years from 2001 thru 2008 – the Bush years - sure looks like those were the years with the lowest unemployment. I don't remember that headline?!? One may wonder what happened in 2007 that really caused the steep climb. What changed? As we saw earlier, could it be that the democrats took control of the congress in Jan 2007 and implemented the same policies they tried during the Carter years? Ironically, that is when the economy tanked, deficits soared, unemployment skyrocketed - once the policies of the democrat controlled Congress took effect in 2007.

But I am getting ahead of myself - Look at the chart above As a result of the Clinton recession and the Sept 2001 attack, the year 2002 was not a good year for America and unemployment jumped. But improvements that started in 2003, really ramped up in 2004 – and unemployment dropped year after year in 2005, 2006, and 2007.

Likewise, you may be wondering what happened in 1996 that seemed to cause unemployment to drop below 5% for the first time in decades. Again, it was a shift in the control of congress – this time Republicans took control.

Moving On…

Just before Obama was elected in November 2008, unemployment had jumped from 6.1% in August and September to 6.5% in October. A huge jump – considering the majority of the previous three years had an average unemployment of 4.7% or less! In fact, prior to that, it was below 6% for 58 consecutive months – beginning in September 2003 (at the end of the Clinton Recession.) Impressed? Look at the unusually low unemployment numbers for the years 2006 and 2007:

Year	Jan	Feb	Mar	Apr	May	Jun	Jul	Aug	Sep	Oct	Nov	Dec
2006	4.7	4.8	4.7	4.7	4.6	4.6	4.7	4.7	4.5	4.4	4.5	4.4
2007	4.6	4.5	4.4	4.5	4.4	4.6	4.7	4.6	4.7	4.7	4.7	5.0

Now remember, the Democrats won the elections in November 2006, winning control of both the House and Senate. They were sworn in January 2007 and their policies and new budget go "full force" by October 2007. And the results were obvious –within 12 months, the "new leadership" in congress saw chronically low 4.7% unemployment shoot up to 5.8% by July 2008.

Year	Jan	Feb	Mar	Apr	May	Jun	Jul	Aug	Sep	Oct	Nov	Dec
2008	5.0	4.9	5.1	5.0	5.4	5.6	5.8	6.1	6.1	6.5	6.8	7.3

Next, we will see the unemployment rate continued to climb, and the Democrats continued to control both the House and the Senate. Due to the "super majority" the Democrats had, hundreds of bills were passed into law, while the republicans could only watch. In some cases, backroom deals, and "pass it before you read it" bills flew through in lightning speed. The results:

Year	Jan	Feb	Mar	Apr	May	Jun	Jul	Aug	Sep	Oct	Nov	Dec
2009	7.8	8.3	8.7	8.9	9.4	9.5	9.5	9.6	9.8	10.0	9.9	9.9
2010	9.7	9.8	9.8	9.9	9.6	9.4	9.5	9.6	9.5	9.5	9.8	9.4
2011	9.1	9.0	8.9	9.0	9.0	9.1	9.1	9.1	9.0	8.9	8.7	8.5
2012	8.3	8.3	8.2	8.1	8.2							

In November 2010, the Republicans gained a majority in the House, while the Senate remained in the control of the democrats. The House passed numerous jobs bills, budgetary appropriation bills, and significant bills to finally restore a competitive edge to American business in an increasingly competitive world. Harry Reid in the Senate blocked them all. In a weird dynamic, Obama blames Republicans in Congress for blocking progress, when in reality; the party blocking everything is his own party – led by Harry Reid in the Senate. The press NEVER points this out.

Average Unemployment Rate by President

Obama (2009-2012) – **9.1%**

Bush (2001-2008) – 5.3%

Clinton (1993-2000) – 5.2%

Bush Sr. (1989-1992) – 6.3%

Reagan (1981-1988) – 7.5%

Carter (1977-1980) – 6.5%

Ford (1974-1977) – 7.2%

Nixon (1969-1974) – 5.1%

Johnson (1963-1968) – 4.4%

Kennedy (1961-1962) – 6.1%

Eisenhower (1953-1960) – 4.9%

The Bottom line is that while each of the last several presidents entered office with un-employment on the rise – each one was able to turn it around quickly… until Obama's term. Keep in mind, that Obama and the Democrats had a super majority in congress when he entered office. The Democrats passed hundreds of bills and Obama signed them – Republicans could only watch. And everyone agrees, regardless of political background, that the recession Reagan inherited was so much worse than the one Obama inherited. Interest rates were 18%, Inflation was through the roof – and I bought a brand new 1980 motorcycle as it was lighter to push while waiting in the gasoline lines.

But as we will see, the *lower unemployment* under Obama Legacy Building is moving ahead!

Average Weeks Unemployed

All presidents since the 80s entered office with the economy in or near recession. All presidents faced natural disasters like hurricanes, flooding, fires, etc. Each president had to deal with the Middle East Conflict, other regional wars, North Korea issues, fluctuating gasoline prices, and sunspots. All presidents have to deal with Congress – even when Congress is led by the opposite party. All very typical issues – all presidents face these types of problems. All presidents are given a grace period of 6-12 months where they are not held accountable for what happens – in other words, they can blame the previous administrations. Beyond 12 months, they own everything that happens. Let's look at the duration of unemployment. The next chart from the BLS, shows the average number of weeks a person stays on unemployment benefits since 1986. It's nauseating to hear anyone say we are moving in the right direction:

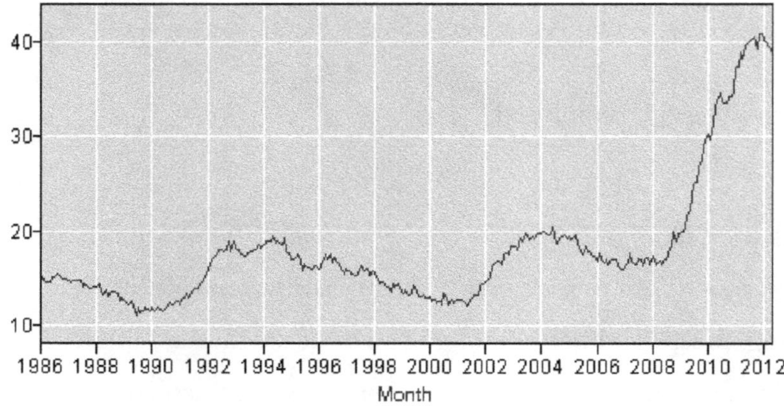

Average Weeks of Unemployment by President

Obama (2009-2012)	33.3 weeks unemployment
Bush (2001 – 2008)	17.3 weeks unemployment
Clinton (1993-2000)	15.8 weeks unemployment
Bush (1989-1992)	13.8 weeks unemployment
Reagan (1981-1988)	15.7 weeks unemployment
Carter (1977-1980)	12.2 weeks unemployment

Obama used his super majority in Congress to do other things…Some states will now pay up to two years of unemployment. Some predict the 2013 average will exceed 52 weeks!

Total Americans employed

Presidents are measured by the total number of Americans working. This is a very easy to understand measurement – How many Americans are working? Today (June 2012) there are a total of 134 million Americans are working – so Obama has a net loss of jobs. You do the simple math. Hear those facts anywhere? Do you ever hear the press challenge assertions around creating whatever the claim is that particular day - Whether the claim is 2 million, 4 million, or 10 million jobs "created or saved"? Think about other presidents and if you think they would be allowed to deceive Americans like this? Would the press just sit there? Would the press challenge claims like these?

Number of Americans Unemployed

This chart shows the number of Americans unemployed per year over the last 35 years. It basically speaks for itself!

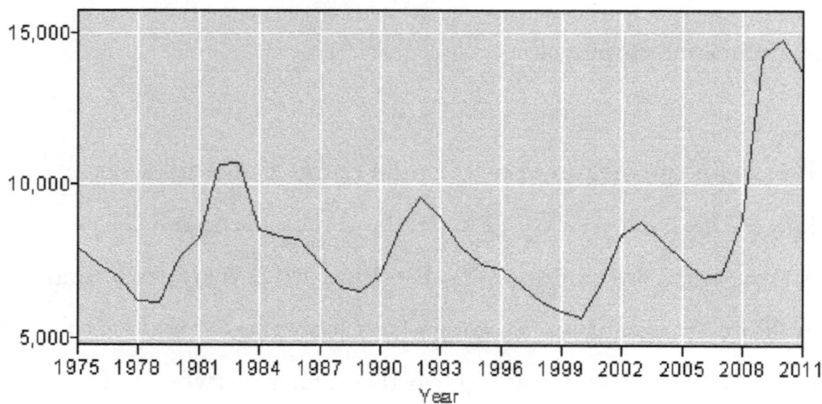

December 2008 – 8,924,000 Americans un-employed

December 2011 – 13,747,000 Americans un-employed

4,823,000 more Americans unemployed after 3 years!

Change … you can believe we do not need!

Preemptive Counter Argument

"You can't blame Clinton for the bad jobs data 21 months into the Bush Administration."

Then please tell me how you try to blame Bush for bad jobs data 40 months (so far) into the Obama years?

CHAPTER 5

HEALTHCARE

Americans were told The Affordable Care Act would:

1. Eliminate the number of Americans without health insurance
2. Reduce healthcare costs for Americans and U.S. government
3. Reduce or eliminate fraud and abuse (stop laughing)

Logically, it is incredible that the U.S. press doesn't challenge the premise:

35 million additional people will somehow have insurance

No additional costs, no reduction in service?

This is ridicules!

Do not lose sight of the main reason there so many Americans have no health insurance.

They cannot afford it.

Anyone with a good job either receives insurance through their employer (primarily paid for by the employer) or they pay for a policy "out-of-pocket". Very few are "free riders" who wait to get sick or need surgery – mooching off the rest of those with insurance. Anyone in upper middle class and certainly the wealthy have Medical Insurance. Most uninsured are poor Americans!

Looking at it another way, where has this concept of providing any service to 35 million additional people (no cost/no impact) ever logically made sense?

Think about it - is this even reasonable?

Could you add service to 35 million Americans with no cost or reduction in service:

- Cable or Satellite TV
- Mail/Package Delivery – government (USPS) or private (UPS, FedEx)
- Rail service
- Car Insurance
- High speed Internet

- Education
- Electricity
- Milk Delivery

Of course not! And it won't work with healthcare! The cost will be immense! And since the government pays (overpays) by an average of 2x or 3x … my goodness.

And who can point to ***any other area*** where the government does something better than private industry? Examining a few examples where both private business and government "compete":

1. Mail Delivery – in both cases, customers pay for the service:
    a. UPS, FedEx, and many other privates earn profits efficiently and expand.
    b. The U.S. Postal service loses money, and needs to close unused facilities.
2. TV/Radio – in both cases, some service is offered free
    a. Private TV or radio – profitable by selling ad time to sponsors (commercials)
    b. Public TV/Radio – usually drain tax money, not profitable, fail often

But Alan – is "profit" the driving factor you ask? Good question!

No, but profit means the service will be around now and in the future. You cannot keep pouring money into such large programs!

To be able to endure, the program must be self-sustainable; or at least mostly self-sustainable! Oh sure, governments can pour money into wasteful and failing endeavors – it's not their money. My question is:

Wasn't "lowering costs" a major reason for doing this?

"Since we already have unused buildings and line ropes, it make sense to me. Hush! I am trying to make this look like heart medication. What'd you think?

I listed the three main reasons for healthcare reform.

1. Eliminate the number of Americans without health insurance
2. Reduce healthcare costs for Americans and U.S. government
3. Reduce or eliminate fraud and abuse

Americans were not sold a massive new government program!

Look what had to happen to pass the law:

- Sold to Americans as a penalty / Argued to Supreme Court as a tax
- Required shady behind closed door deals traded for votes from Democrats –
    - Cornhusker Kickback (removed or re-instated?)
    - "Louisiana Purchase" will give Louisiana extra $4.3 Billion
    - Massachusetts Benefits From Loophole While Rest Of Country Loses Out
- Waivers were granted to Unions and companies friendly with Obama Administration
- Super Majority (Democrats) prevented normal debate
- Super Majority (Democrats) prevented public vetting by Americans
- Pelosi "pass it before we can read it" approach reeked of corruption
- Cost underestimated – actually cost triple Obama's 2009 projection
- The You Can Keep your Doctor Pledge – removed
- The You Can Keep Your Insurance Pledge – removed
- Medicare – Democrats cut $500 billion reducing Seniors care

- Republicans blocked from adding amendment to protect Medicare
- "Free Screenings" – actually only available at "Health Fairs"

Does anyone really believe we will accomplish any of the 3 goals?

1. Eliminate the number of Americans without health insurance
2. Reduce healthcare costs for Americans and U.S. government
3. Reduce or eliminate fraud and abuse

It's obvious that reasons number 2 and number 3 are … well let's just say it – absolutely absurd!

That leaves reason number 1 – Eliminate the number of Americans without Health Insurance. Remember, it is unacceptable to reduce the number by a few percentage points – normal business cycles would accomplish that, without sacrificing care or spending trillions of additional taxpayer money. No – the goal must be to eliminate the un-insured.

How's that going so far? Let's do the research, and fill in the form:

Bush Sr. - ____________________________ million uninsured

Clinton - ___________________________ million uninsured

Bush Jr. - ____________________________ million uninsured

Obama - ___________________________ million uninsured

My research says that - two years after ObamaCare was signed into law there is a record high number of uninsured – 51 million Americans without Insurance (and climbing fast as of this writing).

"Get your free screenings as part of the new Healthcare Law" says the commercial. But there it was, at the bottom of the TV screen. There was the "fine print". It didn't say I could get a free screening from my doctor. It didn't say I could get my screening at a facility near my home. It said the screening was "participating providers only".

What does that mean?

In Atlanta, once or twice a year, a Free Clinic opens up for a few days at the Georgia dome to provide healthcare (and occasionally dental care) to local residents. Most cannot afford insurance and do not receive company based coverage. Lines wrap around the building, you wait for hours, if not days…and eventually you see a doctor. Is this where I get my free screening?

In fact, I'd love to hear from people who actually have "free screenings" from their doctor. And I will tell you why… each time someone mentions a "free screening" they imply the new Healthcare law is the reason it's available. So far, every case shows that's not true. For example, I was told free colonoscopy screenings were NOW available at Grady Hospital in Atlanta. When I checked into it, I found out that Grady has offered this type of "free screenings" for years – long before Obama was president.

So let me know – AFTER you check your facts!

By the way - wouldn't every president have done the same exact thing? To pay for this program, taxes will go up for all Americans. Seniors are the big losers! Many have already lost their coverage, companies and unions have waivers, and the number of uninsured is increasing at an unprecedented rate. Regardless of the way the new Healthcare program was sold, the reality is:

1. Medicare was slashed $500 billion – reduction in service for all seniors
2. Many are losing their coverage
3. Many can no longer go to their family doctor
4. Doctors are refusing patients on Medicare
5. Routine Services no longer covered
6. Two tier system is forming:
    a. Premium coverage – Clooney, Oprah, Warren Buffet, and other wealthy
    b. Pool – the rest of Americans will fight for basic services and scarce resources
7. Seniors services are being squeezed to make room for others
8. Seniors encouraged to go on Food Stamps - "Obama Senior Healthy Eating Plan"
9. Quality of care is deteriorating - to make room for 35 – 50 million people

Remember when the rest of the world envied the U.S. Education System? Not anymore. Are we going to see American healthcare move down on list as well?

Healthcare Talking Points

Democrats are well prepared! Watching the Sunday Talk shows in July 2012, we heard repetition:

- ✓ 17 million NOW insured
- ✓ Millions of College kids NOW insured
- ✓ No one is denied insurance NOW
- ✓ 99% pay nothing - free medical care for all!

Does anyone really believe 17 million of the millions uninsured now have insurance? Which means only 18 million are now uninsured? No – it's 51 million uninsured and climbing fast!

I should mention that most were very careful to say the specific talking point – "may" "soon" "possibly". But others later changed those same words to "is" "now" "definitely"… when repeating the false claims.

Healthcare - In Conclusion

Have no doubt – Obama's Legacy will be that he provided health insurance to all Americans. And his legacy will be that everyone benefits - seniors, students, middle class, poor and rich all have better, less expensive healthcare. Thanks to the Affordable Care Act – commonly called ObamaCare! The way I see it, there are 2 options:

1. Law stays and healthcare declines with costs skyrocketing
2. Law is overturned – Republicans are vilified for taking away care for women, students, minorities, seniors, and poor

It's a win/win situation regardless of the results! No one will ever look back and compare the quality, cost, or overall benefits lost if the program remains. Good intentions, bad results? This is really just a shift – Senior citizens loose services, so 18-26 year old can be insured? We all will see our quality of care decrease substantially. By the way, that is why Congress has their own medical plan – and their plan is awesome!

The Legacy around healthcare is solid!

CHAPTER 6

INTERNATIONAL DISASTER

Legacy Building around International Affairs is difficult – and really not essential.

Most Americans would be surprised – no shocked – at how different the rest of the world views American Presidents. Today it's quite easy to search for articles online. You can pull up news reports and other articles from news organizations in other countries.

The world sees Americans Presidents … very differently. And just because the U.S. media says a U.S. president is either adored or despised – the opposite may be the truth! I will let you do the research on international perspectives on Presidents.

It just seems that many of the gains made during hawkish admirations, are given back during the less hawkish administrations… and then some.

For example, from 2002 – 2008, amazing progress was made in regions of the world that most had given up on. In fact, just a few years earlier, most would have never thought elections could be held in places such as Iraq and Afghanistan. No doubt these elections caused the Arab Spring (but let's be careful not to give Bush any credit here wink wink). And who really believed that any progress could be made in places like Somalia, or in the Philippines where terror group Abu Sayyaf was hunted down and basically exterminated. (Covert ops rule!)

Well within 3 years –

- Afghanistan has taken a huge slide backwards
- Israel has been thrown under the bus
- Lebanon has reversed all the progress made
- Iran has brazenly attempted assassinations – right here in the U.S.
- Russia basically took over part of Georgia
- Syria *was* isolated and Hilary Clinton suggested was ready to flip (away from Iran)
- Iraq may be the scariest. Obama rushed out U.S. forces for political reasons and over the objection of military leaders. As warned, the vacuum was filled quickly by Iran. If Iranian influence continues to grow, the transition to democracy in Iraq may be completely lost. In fact, the situation is much dire – the "and then some" is devastating as we slide back

over 30 years! A little history should help to make it clearer. You see for over 30 years the U.S. has worked hard to make sure that neither Iraq nor Iran gained control of the majority of Middle Eastern oil. During the 1980s, when Iran and Iraq were at war, to ensure that neither Iraq nor Iran defeated the other, the U.S. strategy was a stalemate, and we assisted each country to make sure it was a stalemate with no clear winner. We saw major disadvantages if Iraq won, and an even worse scenario with Iran winning. So the U.S. provided aid and intelligence to make sure neither side won. If they now become buddies, and view the U.S. as their enemy, then we are back to the situation we had in the 80s.

- North Korea "snookered" the Obama team into restoring the aid (cutoff by Bush)
- Egypt was a friendly dictatorship… peace with Israel and U.S. No one seems to know what to expect now
- Upset trading partners worldwide – lack of understanding
- Cutting U.S. weapons (without similar cuts by Russia)

A few examples of some of the "and then some" loses:

- We supported the overthrow of friendly dictators (Egypt, Libya)
- We did not support the overthrow of enemy dictators (Iran, Syria)
- North Korea has U.S. funding again. Will enhance and sell missiles to Iran, Pakistan, Hamas…

- Drone technology – let it "gently" land in Iran rather than destroy it
- Helicopter Stealth Technology (live video feed showed tail intact – we watched them take it!)

Dictators are bad. But there are "friendly dictators" and there are "enemy dictators". Why did we support the uprisings in countries that were ruled by "friendly dictators"? Yet, we not only refused to support uprisings in Iran and Syria ("enemy dictators"), but we announced to the world that we would not provide any help. Thousands were slaughtered and the uprising in Iran faded. In Egypt and Libya we gave full support. Why? Who thought this through?

History shows that during Republican administrations, the U.S. tends to have strong international policies. During Republican administrations, democracy usually expands, hostages are released, and the International community respects America; even if they don't agree with us.

During Carter, Clinton, and now Obama administrations, you may have noticed hearing about Americans being captured and held hostage overseas. The Carter years produced the Iranian hostages. 52 Americans were held hostage for 444 days from November 4, 1979, to January 20, 1981 – released the very day Reagan was sworn in as president. (Some say that shortly after Reagan was elected in Nov 1980, he threatened to attack and occupy Iran. History shows that the Iranians were afraid of Reagan – but not militarily. They knew that Reagan would not negotiate – and since Carter saw it as the only possible way he had a chance to win the election in 1980, he was willing to do anything to get the hostages free. In the months leading up to the election, Carter starting offering basically everything the Iranians had been demanding for over a year – in a desperate attempt to change what seemed to be a terrible defeat at the polls. He gave the Iranians most of what they demanded, but it was too late as he lost the election

During the Clinton years, hostages were taken in several countries with most being released after ransom was paid or prisoners were released. It seemed that the lack of response to all the attacks on Americans worldwide, and other hostage taking embolden the bad guys. And so far, during the Obama term, hostages have been taken:

- Iran - (3 students hiking in 2009, and 1 retired FBI agent)
- Somalia - two aid workers. One was American Jessica Buchanan.
- Cuba - one hostage (Alan Gross) taken in 2009
- Egypt – 19 Americans including Sam LaHood (son of Transportation Secretary LaHood)
- Somalia – Four on yacht held and killed in Feb 2011

There have been rumors of what may have been traded for the student hikers – it may be a few more years before we really know. As of this writing, the others are still being held. Cuba recently asked Senator Leahy to trade Gross for a bunch of U.S. prisoners.

To be fair, Reagan did struggle with hostage taking in Lebanon and a terrible U.S. barracks bombing. History shows that Iran was behind both the bombing and the group who took the hostages. More on Iran in a little bit. Cater, like Clinton in the 1990s, appeared to dismiss enemies when they vowed to destroy the U.S. and friends. Attacks during the Carter years culminated with the Iranian hostages. The attacks during the Clinton years culminated in the attacks on 9/11. In hindsight, the failed Lebanon policies of the 1980s were a result of indecision. When it came to Lebanon, it was basically a proxy war between the U.S. and Iran. We were not "all in", and we were not "all out". We straddled the fence and you cannot do that when extremists are determined. In the case of Lebanon, soldiers, weapons, and training easily traveled from Iran through Syria into Lebanon.

During the 1980s the U.S. military complex was rebuilt after decades of decay. America's reputation as a strong world leader was restored. But that changed in the 1990s. After a string of unanswered attacks on the U.S. and U. S. facilities worldwide year after year, terror groups felt invincible. They became bolder and financing from Iran and wealthy extremists groups increased significantly allowing much more sophisticated attacks. Attacks that, only a few years earlier would have been considered fantasy other than in James Bond movies, could now be pursued since American Leadership had gone soft. Attacks that require significant planning for years, overseas training, and taking up residency in the USA could now be accomplished since Americans were considered "sleeping at the switch" in regard to security. Political Correctness was the theme and terrorists used the new "open door" policies of the 1990s to their advantage. Unfortunately, emboldened by the lack of response through the 90s, the terrorists hit hard on September 11th, 2001.

Iran

History will show that Iran is responsible for many of the world problems. Trillions are spent globally on security that would not be necessary if Iran did not exist. That is not to say that the Iranian people are all radical extremists. In fact, prior to the radical overthrow of the Shaw in the 1970s, Iran was considered by Middle Eastern standards as a multi-cultural country, governed by mostly moderates. The extremists Shiites in power in Iran for the last 30 years are wealthy extremist radicals that are not tolerant of anyone who is not also as extreme. A moderate Muslim is no less a traitor than a Christian, Hindi, or Jew when it comes to the Wahhabis beliefs of the current Iranian leadership. So while they may be "friendly" with other not so extreme groups while wreaking havoc on America and our allies, eventually, the moderates will be targeted as well. It truly is their way or the highway. There is no coexisting with theses extremists.

Nobody knows for sure – both everyone agrees that the number of dead Americans in Afghanistan and Iraq would be less than half – if not for the direct efforts of Iran.

Billions are spent maintaining armies that are in place because of Iran. Neighboring nations are either spending billions to build up military assets because of Iran, or expecting protection from the U.S.

Billions are being spent to develop and deploy sophisticated missile defense technology because of Iran. Billions are being spent on short and long term medical care of Americans killed or wounded because of Iran. Millions are spent to develop armored vehicles and body armor to defend against powerful IEDs built and supplied by Iran. Weapons systems are being acquired by nations – some nations that we would rather did not have the weapons; because of Iran. The main problem in dealing with the current leadership in Iran is they simply do not care about long term implications or ramifications. They are not concerned with the long term … at all. Why should they be? They are mad men who welcome death soon – and will gladly see Iran destroyed in response to detonating a nuclear weapon in America or Israel.

So called "crippling sanctions that will take decades to recover from…" is, well … unimportant if your plan is for a devastating response from the world that causes the complete destruction of your county; the land now called Iran. To the extremists, this is nirvana! This is Heaven! This is the ultimate goal! They simply laugh when someone points out that Iran should cease all efforts to build nuclear military capabilities so they can "rejoin the international community before it is too late". To the extremists this is a joke! The extremists fully expect to use a nuclear weapon in an attack on the USA or Israel in the next year – two years at the latest. So who cares about the long term affects sanctions may have in 10 years…

In 2009, millions of Iranians took to the street demanding regime change, but ultimately the uprising was cruelly suppressed and many Iranians were tortured and executed. According to statistics from the Islamic regime's Justice Department, all Iranian prisons are overflowing and there is a need for more prisons. As reported by Iranian officials, last year alone more than 600 people were executed, including women.

Most of the rockets that hit Israel each day – average 30 to 50 each and every day – are paid for and supplied by Iran. The world funds the IEDs and rockets that kill Americans every week thru Iranian oil sales. Higher oil prices mean more weapons. Sanctions have no impact because those who buy from Iran will look elsewhere for oil. Countries like China, Russia, and others less friendly to the USA, will gladly buy the extra oil from Iran. The only effect oil sanctions on Iran will cause will be a shifting of vendors/suppliers globally. No big deal – like going to Loews or Target instead of Home Depot or Kmart…

By not properly using the assets in the area to keep Iran in check over the past couple years, Iran was allowed to move forward with both their nuclear and missile programs. History will show that the last couple years were the "shut up or put up" years regarding Iran and the U.S. leadership chose to "shut up". One thing is for sure – this is not going to end well!

Iraq

Democrats try to argue that the main, and in some cases the only, reason the U.S. went to war in Iraq was because Iraq may still have WMDs. Really? The WMDs concern was like 8th on the Top 10 Reasons List.

In fact, had WMDs never been mentioned… we would have gone to war in Iraq. There were so many more important reasons. It was the right thing to do.

By 2003, Iraq had become the most destabilizing country in the world. Period! Some will try to argue that Iran and North Korea are more destabilizing. That may be true now, but that was not true in 2003.

I will spare you the long drawn out history. In brief, Iraq wanted to control Middle Eastern oil. Had Iraq been successful in the late 1990s and held Kuwait, who they had conquered with barely a shot fired, there would have been no stopping them. Smaller countries with no army to defend themselves would fold like Kuwait. Even those with large U.S. bases, would have given in to Saddam's demands to pay Iraq royalties on their oil revenue. Eventually, Saudi Arabia would cave. Do you think Saddam Hussein was mad? Do you think Saddam Hussein held a grudge against the U.S.? Saddam was 80% of the way to his goal of dominance over the Middle East. After the U.S. steps in in January 1991 ousting Iraq from Kuwait, and

Saddam is back to 40% toward his dream. Saddam was mad - while he let the Iraqi people starve, he used the countries oil revenue to lash out at the U.S. and our allies, every way he could.

- By 2003, Iraq had become the Number One exporter of terrorism – with the possible exception of Iran. In truth, by 2003 Iraq and Iran were in a "deadly competition" to see who could kill the most Americans worldwide. It was like they try to up each other-
    - number killed
    - sophistication of the attack
    - attack U.S. property or citizens in or near the U.S. mainland
    - money and weapons given to al Qaeda Hamas, Hezbollah, and others
    - rewards paid to families of suicide bombers (of Americans or friends)
    - U.S. military planes shot at (Iraq)
- By 2003, Iraq had attempted to assassinate former president Clinton – and the only reason it failed was because those chosen to carry it out made mistakes.
- By 2003, Iraq was using its huge oil revenue to fund terror groups in neighboring countries such as Turkey, Saudi Arabia, United Emirates, Qatar, and Yemen. (while Iraqi citizens starved)
- By 2003, Iraq attempted to shoot down American military plans every few weeks.

- By 2003, the safe havens in Afghanistan, Somalia, and the southern Philippines were no longer available due to the brave men and women in the U.S. military. Iraq became the new destination.
- By 2003, Iraq refused to turn over international criminals and terrorists, who were openly living in Iraq – and in some cases, living very comfortably as guests of the Iraqi government.
- By 2003, Iraq was sending a steady stream of thugs, weapons, and money, thru Jordan, to terror camps in the West Bank and Gaza strip.
- By 2003, Iraq was meeting with scientist from Pakistan (Khan) and other countries in an attempt to acquire nuclear technology.
- By 2003, Iraqis neighbors and all nearby countries agreed to remove the brutal dictator's regime.

Oh yeah, and by the way, by 2003, most of the world believed that Iraq may have WMDS leftover from the 1980s and 1990s – and they may give those WMDs to their new friends, to be used in attacks on Americans. With or without WMDs – we had no choice. In fact, if evidence was submitted to the U.N. that Iraq didn't have any leftover WMDs, nothing would have changed. The U.S., U.K., and several others argued a long list of reasons to attack Iraq – removing any single item would have had the same effect – NONE!

And, after the brutal regime was ousted, seeing Iraqis proudly show-off their "purple inked thumbs" after voting in the 1st real elections … made removing that brutal regime worth it. History may rewrite these facts, but –

- ✓ Iraqis loved America and Americans in 2004 and 2005 for freeing them
- ✓ Iraqis proudly raised the U.S. flag along with the Iraqi flag
- ✓ Iraqis rejected external and internal terror groups after Hussein's ouster
- ✓ Iraqis elections were broadcast worldwide and inspired others
- ✓ Iraq allowed U.S. bases to be established in Iraq (all eyes on Iran)

More importantly, the stage was set – the people of Iran and Syria would rise up in years after the liberation of Iraq. Unfortunately for the people of Iran, American leadership changed in the 2008 U.S. elections. Rather than support the uprisings in Iran – whose people expressed a desire to part with their extreme ways since the 1980s, and rejoin the world of civilized nations – the new Administration stood by and watched the Iranian army slaughter thousands of people. How do you think the Syria uprising would have turned out had the Iranian uprising been supported?

Lastly, as a result of the Iraq war - Libya gave up their nuclear weapons program. And we now know that most Iraqis WMDs were transported to Syria!

Israel

No country has been thrown under the bus more than Israel. It is as though Obama is following a list given to him by leaders of Iran, Syria, al Qaeda, Hamas, and Hezbollah. What would that list look like?

- Overthrow leaders of countries with "friendly ties" to Israel Egypt, Libya
- Install radical extremist led governments
- Pressure remaining leaders to end Israelis ties (Jordan, Turkey, etc.)
- Reverse democratic reforms in Iraq
- Force U.S. out of Afghanistan and Iraq (such that U.S. is viewed as an enemy of Islam)
- Crush dissent in countries such as Iran, Syria, and Lebanon
- Take U.S. hostages – bargain for computer virus fix
- Determine time, route and bases required of Israel's planned attack on nuclear plant
- Trick U.S. into reversing a 50 year policy – 1967 borders

Let us look at this in a different way… shall we? Looking back over 3½ years it seems that Obama is indeed following a plan that would put Israel in a very bad position. Is the plan to hope that Iran doesn't (directly or through a proxy) use a nuclear weapon once they have one? Who believes Iran would go through all they have – to what, stockpile weapons? Please? Remember that al Qaeda threatened to attack America years before they had trained pilots and committed the attacks of September 11th – America didn't take them serious no matter how matter Americans were killed throughput the 1990s. Likewise, Iranian extremists who now control the government in Iran have vowed to destroy America, Israel, and allies. Ignoring this threat will result in a nuclear explosion….

We are now faced with the choice to attack or hope the nuclear explosion is a small one.

What is the downside to an Israelis attack? There is not a downside. Today, Iran is building and shipping as many missiles possible – that are then launched into Israel every single day. They are killing as many Americans possible in Afghanistan, Iraq, Somalia, and elsewhere around the world.

There is no downside! Iran is doing everything they can today. To be sure, they are full steam ahead and have no capacity to "ramp up".

Afghanistan

End the war? Or surrender the gains?

Why did we enter Afghanistan? We wanted to disrupt the terrorists there so they would not be able to attack the U.S. mainland or around the world. We attacked because America was attacked, year after year, by a group of terrorists based in and protected by the Afghanistan government. The group attacked the WTC in 1993, attacked two U.S. embassies in Aug 1998, the Cole off Somalia in 2000, assassinated numerous American diplomats, and many others.

We entered Afghanistan to end the attacks – once and for all. We planned to stay for a very long time. We spent billions of dollars and years building America's largest overseas military base in the world. This base has more to do with Iran than anything else.

Democrats call it an "unfunded war".

1. It wouldn't have been necessary if Clinton didn't shun his responsibility
2. I would rather see $$ spent to respond to 9/11 than ignore the attack
3. How many Americans had to die to call it a "funded war"
4. Defense of America is the number one Federal responsibility
5. Giving $$ to Obama supporters' companies is "funded" but protecting America is "not funded"
6. Had a democrat president been in office on 9/11 – would he have defended America?
7. Democrats concerned about $$ spent after 9/11 – but $$ wasted on failed green technology okay
8. The "unfunded war" crowd is never concerned about funding for Social Security, Medicare, and Medicaid

9. Why are military $$ so scrutinized – but wasted $$ EVERYWHERE else is ignored

In reality, Afghanistan was simply being used as "launching pad" by Iran to attach America, Israel, and our allies. They funded the terrorists in Afghanistan (and still do), and provided training and other expertise. (The IED's that killed and maimed most Americans in Iraq – also came directly from Iran or with Iran's assistance.)

Listen, let me be blunt, if you call Afghanistan "an unfunded war" you are telling me you would have allowed the attacks on September 11th, without response - like we did year after year during the Clinton Administration. And that "costs" should have been considered to determine if we should response to the killing of 3000 Americans.

Amazing how those who question spending $$ to make sure another 9/11 never happens again – the unfunded war they call it – are the same people with no concern about the billions wasted trying to power cars with seaweed, bee larva, and kudzu plants.

Quick note about bin Laden

Imagine the reports if Obama had passed on the opportunity to send the Special Forces team into Pakistan take out Osama bin Laden?

I am shocked when I hear that it was a "brave" decision to go after bin Laden. Did Obama really have a choice? History will show that bin Laden's location was confirmed months earlier. News reports a week or so before the raid, indicated that bin Laden was in Pakistan, and that the Pakistanis were considering "giving him up". In reality, bin Laden had been under a form of house arrest for years in Pakistan – rarely seeing the light of day. His health and mental faculties had deteriorated significantly, and he longer led any terror groups or had anything to do with attacks. He was obsessed with creating his own persona and legacy – and ironically spent most of the day watching U.S. television stations. He was barely able to walk for more than a few minutes – and certainly wasn't worried about U.S. forces seeing him out in the courtyard. U.S. Forces were hundreds of miles away and were certainly not looking for anyone in the shadow of a large Pakistani Military Base complex and training Facility.

I am glad the brave U.S. Special Forces were given the chance, and took out bin Laden. But let's not lose sight of the fact that bin Laden was a feeble, mentally unstable, dying man. In the bigger picture his death, over a decade after 9/11, has unfortunately no impact on the War on Terrorism. Most of the al Qaeda group was decimated by 2007 – those left have either joined other groups – like Al-Shabaab, Hamas, Hezbollah, Muslim Brotherhood, Abu Sayyaf, etc. – or have transitioned into primarily focused on the heroin drug trade.

Drones killing women\children (is not a recruiting tool)

Obama and democrats argue that it is torture to pour water on terrorists. "It is a recruitment tool for al Qaeda", Obama said in several speeches in 2008. Now fast forward to 2012. Drones are used extensively to kill terrorists in Pakistan. And in many of those attacks, nearby women and children are also killed. Somehow this is not objectionable to the left in America. Where are all the stars, musicians, and athletes protesting? How is this action not a recruitment tool – but pouring water on 3 or 4 men who proudly admitted to killing Americans – some in the 9/11 attacks – is a recruitment tool? How is this not considered inhumane? After signing an Executive Order in 2012, Obama now has the ability to use drones to attack EVEN if the ID of the terrorists in unconfirmed. Please don't confuse what I am highlighting here – as I actually agree with drone attacks, scaring "proud terrorists" with water, and even covert ops inside Pakistan, Iran, Syria, and North Korea.

My point is – people on the left hung Bush in effigy – for ordering the water scaring treatment on 3 or 4 hardcore terrorist leaders. Taking out families that may also include a terrorist or two hasn't caused any protests from the left, no Congressional Hearings; Alex Baldwin hasn't left the country…

CHAPTER 7

GASOLINE PRICES

"Gas prices have dropped dramatically over the last 2 weeks – now averaging $3.20 - $3.40 per gallon", was how the enthusiastic reporter stated it - as the July 4th 2012 week approached. She was smiling, and happy! Contrast that to the reports in 2007 when gas was less than $2.00 a gallon. Reports then said it was obvious Bush had "sold out the country to enrich his oil pals".

It is truly shameful – the extent of the bias in the media!

When I was growing up, I joined the band and tried to play several instruments – trumpet, violin, and drums. I really wasn't that good at any of them – because I wasn't really interested in playing in the band. It's amazing how - when you really do not want to do something, how you put little effort into it, resist advice from others, and usually see little success. Family and friends tried to help – they advised me to seek out suggestions from others who played in the school band, the local Fire Department band, music clubs/groups, and research at the library. All great suggestions! The problem was …I really didn't want to be in the band.

This is what Obama is doing in regard to gasoline prices.

Based on the steps taken by the Obama Administrations so far, it seems to me that lower gasoline prices are certainly not a goal of the Obama Administration. And, the person Obama put in charge of the Energy Department has stated several times that higher gasoline prices is his goal – and has been for years. The way Energy Secretary Chu sees it:

Low gasoline prices deter innovation in green technology.

In March 2012, Energy Secretary Chu was asked a direct question in a Congressional hearing "Is the goal of the Energy Department to lower gasoline prices?" He said "No!" When asked a second time, he made it clear that he understood the question the 1st time – and stated that the goal of the Energy Department under the Obama Administration was to lower consumption of gasoline. (A few weeks later, he attempted to clarify his answers saying that "of course" lower gasoline prices were a goal.) Check out the YouTube video and tell me what you think.

I watched the replay of the hearing – I walked away thinking Chu was pouting that the oil industry had an overwhelming head start on alternative energy industries and should be punished. He admitted that most green technology (seaweed, bee larva, kudzu) simply doesn't work. He begrudgingly accepted that, until innovation creates a REAL alternative to oil, the American economy is dependent on oil. He did not seem happy!

And if it doesn't bother Americans that they are suffering high gasoline prices, in a sense, to conduct a social experiment around energy while the Energy Department is ignoring America's primary source of energy (oil); then wait till you hear what people over at the EPA think about high gasoline prices. They want to punish oil companies – even though they admit prices will go much higher. A whistle blower leaked a video of someone from the Obama EPA team saying they needed to "crucify" oil companies financially – to set an example. (Gasoline prices would skyrocket under EPA plans.) He actually mentioned how the crusaders would slaughter a few villagers – so the remaining villagers would comply. So help me to understand the logic:

- A one-time release from the Strategic Oil Reserves will reduce gasoline pump prices?
- But consistent, predictable, non-stop drilling will not reduce gasoline pump prices?

Ladies and Gentleman, who wouldn't like to –

- Power cars, planes, trains, and boats with clean technology?
- Heat/cool our homes with clean technology?
- Recharge cell phone, laptops, tablets with clean technology?

But if the technology is not ready – then it's not ready. Let's not destroy America in an effort to force innovation. Believe me, companies like GE, Apple, IBM and others would dive into (and try to dominate) an alternative energy industry – if there was one! The technology is not ready!

The Obama Administration has reversed decisions made in both the Clinton and Bush Administrations to expand off shore drilling. Despite all those cuts on federally owned land, Obama could not stop drilling on private lands – and that drilling continued unabated. In fact, the extra drilling on private land has increased substantially to make up for the cuts by Obama. So the truth is that America is actually drilling more today than ever before, despite Obama's efforts. What would gasoline prices be if we resumed the plans to drill offshore? (BTW - Our neighbors like Mexico and Canada are drilling off shore. Some say that while we bicker, they take the oil.)

The U.S. Government will never invent anything!

Did the U.S. Government invent the iPhone? What about the compact disc? What about the telephone? What about the wheel? Or fire? Hundreds of millions of dollars are being spent around the world to develop a replacement for oil. The brightest minds are involved! Potential profits are unimaginable! The profit motive is the ONLY reason global innovators need!

The U.S. Federal Government will not invent anything – throwing money at it, is a waste!

Gasoline prices have doubled since Obama took office. It's obvious to me that the Obama Administration would prefer higher gasoline prices to encourage innovation, investment, and risk in alternatives to oil. When anyone fairly answers the following two simple questions, it should be abundantly clear.

1. What has Obama done to *increase* domestic oil production?
2. What has Obama done to *decrease* domestic oil production?

Good Intentions, bad results.

In spite of Obama's policies that have greatly reduced areas to drill for oil – America is drilling more than ever – thanks to private land that the president is unable to limit drilling. I believe he would cut back on private land also if he could.

I wonder what gasoline prices would be if Obama didn't block all those areas that were previously open for drilling?

Good Intention	**Bad Result**
Ban oil drilling in Atlantic -	Oil price soar, Iran more $ used for

environment	terror on USA
Ban oil drilling in Gulf of Mexico - environment	Our oil drilled by Mexico and other countries.
Increase taxes on oil companies – oil alternatives	Tax added to price of gasoline – prices rise
Extend unemployment benefits	Delays job search
Harsh regulations on Manufacturing - pollution	Jobs go overseas
Strong banking regulations	Small Business loans evaporate
Provide an alternative source of student loans	Private sources disappear, high interest rates (3x)
New Home loan regulations	Homeownerships rates plummet
Small Business taxes – federal debt	Widespread Small Business layoffs

CHAPTER 8

NATIONAL DEBT

We have already covered quite a bit of material on the U.S. Federal Debt. I wanted to show you one more way of looking at the debt - and why it is critical that the spending STOP!

The last time the debt was this high, as a percentage of GDP, the U.S. was in a depression! Both the Clinton and Bush Recessions would seem like a slow month … in comparison to the 30s and 40s in America!

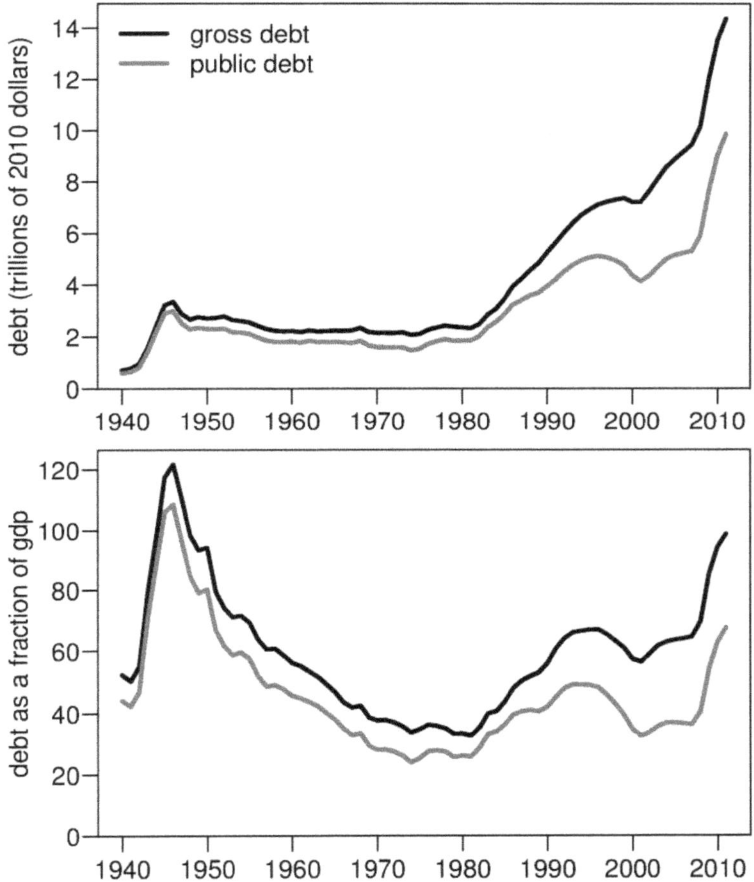

The National Debt Clock (http://www.usdebtclock.org) was a regular fixture on the nightly news when Bush was in office. That was when the debt had reached $7 trillion. Now that it is more than double that amount, it's not important – not newsworthy. In fact, it is rarely reported on the nightly news.

Oh yes, media collusion is critical to Legacy Building!

CHAPTER 9

VOTING RIGHTS

If you think it is okay to vote without identification … then I know with 100% certainty who you will vote for in the 2012 elections… and that is scary!

I cherish my vote. It's all I have. I earned the right to vote – I followed the rules. **I FOLLOWED THE RULES!** My vote is important to me. I respect you, even if voting is a right you do not value. Or if you choose not to vote – that is your right. But don't take my right away. Don't you dare dilute my vote!

If you feel the same way I do about my vote, how would you feel if – after voting, you notice the polling place worker crumble up your ballot and throw it away? Well that is exactly the result... regardless of the intention! Read on...

Go to any civilized country and try to vote without id! How'd that work out for you? The only people in America that cannot show identification to vote are those who:

- Lost the right to vote (prison, revoked citizenship, deported)
- Not a U.S. citizen
- Not in the country legally
- Want to commit fraud – change election by stuffing the ballot box

And guess what? These are people who have not earned the right to vote in U.S. Elections. So, when you hear people use code words like "voter suppression", what they mean is they want to allow ANYONE to vote NUMEROUS times in the U.S. Elections. They want their candidate to win, EVEN if cheating is required! Period!

Oh, by the way, just to show you how dumb politicians think the average Americans is... one proponent of allowing anyone to vote suggested that "the poor in America do not have identification". Maybe that was true in 1940. Items that you must have at least one form of identification:

✓ Apply for a Job	✓ Library Card
✓ Unemployment	✓ Airplane
✓ Rent room / Apartment / House	✓ Enlist
✓ Food stamps	✓ Buy Beer
✓ Disability	✓ Medicare / Medicaid
✓ Bus / Train Card	✓ Adult Education
✓ Visit Doctor / Hospital	✓ Internet Access
✓ Cellular Phone	✓ Prescriptions
✓ Electricity / Water / Natural Gas	✓ Enter most countries
✓ Cable or Satellite TV	✓ Rent a Car
✓ Debit or Credit Card	✓ Other Social Services
✓ Enroll Children in School	✓ Dance Club, Lounge, Casino
	✓ Senior Discount

No, this is about allowing cheating in a U.S. election! It is wrong-

- to encourage those who do not have the right to vote in U.S. elections – to do so
- to allow the people who have not followed the rules to vote!
- to allow those from other countries to vote in U.S. elections

- to allow fraudulently or duplicate votes.

Not One American Vote Diluted – Not One!

A group of Democrats and Republicans decided that, once cast, there was no way to verify questionable ballots. But what about someone who actually shows up to vote without identification? So instead of allowing "ANYONE to vote NUMEROUS times" they suggested:

1. Allow the vote to be cast
2. Put the vote aside
3. Cross reference voting databases to verify validity of voter
4. Once verified, include vote in count

Sounds simple right? And since the number of people in America that would actually show up to vote without identification is, in my opinion less than one tenth of 1% nationwide, the verification would be simple and not time consuming at all! Think about it – this ensures that not one American vote is diluted. Not one American is prevented from voting!

ANYONE WHO SAYS "NO" TO THIS SOLUTION - WANTS TO STEAL ELECTIONS!

Those who "claim" to be concerned with voter's rights – should examine the number of military absentee ballots that are purposefully thrown away every election! The men and women fighting and stationed overseas vote using absentee ballots – hundreds of thousands of military members vote this way. Most experts say that half of them are thrown out – never opened, never counted. When they solve the military vote problem, let me know. Then … we can look at the 1000 or so people nationwide without identification. That will be a relatively simple fix ONCE we fix the military vote problem. On the other hand, if you dismiss the 100,000s of votes sent by the military using absentee ballots – do not expect Americans to take serious your concern with 1000 or so voters. Is Holder concerned with the military votes? Is he suing states to make sure that the absentee ballots are sent out in time? Is he making should the votes of men and women in the U.S. Armed Forces are counted?

Marilyn Monroe and Babe Ruth voted in 2008

Did Donald Duck vote in the 2008 U.S. Presidential elections? Did Marilyn Monroe vote? If so, that would mean my vote counts less? In fact, if ANYONE is able to vote more than once – then my vote will mean less. Seeing the videos of people admitted that they were paid to register names – ANY NAMES – is particularly disturbing in lieu of other seemingly unrelated reports. Those reports say that individuals were given names, and told to go in and out of the polling station and to vote each time using a different name on the list.

ISN'T THIS THE REAL DISENFRANCHISEMENT? My vote counts less if we are allowing Donald Duck to vote – this action would nullify my vote!

Disfranchisement (also called **disenfranchisement**) is the revocation of the right of suffrage (the right to vote) of a person or group of people, or rendering a person's vote less effective, or ineffective. Disfranchisement may occur explicitly through law, or implicitly by intimidation or by placing unreasonable requirements.

Holder has directed the U.S. Department of Justice to:

1. Reverse a guilty verdict in a voter intimidation case
2. Sue states to allow votes to be cast without identification
3. Sue states to prevent them from securing the border

Now, reread the definition:

1. … rendering a person's vote less effective
2. … by intimidation

Holder fought hard to reverse the voter intimidation conviction. This is a picture (below) of the actual intimidation as it was taking place in front of a polling station in 2008 that Holder ordered nullified. Yes, that is a nightstick – IN FRONT OF A U.S. VOTER STATION! Not in 1940 or 1960, this is 2008!

Holder fought the conviction saying the gentlemen in the picture (above) had a right to be there! Holder put the full resources of the DOJ into reversing the guilty verdict.

So now anyone hearing Holder say voters shouldn't need identification – and that making sure every valid vote is counted is his *main* concern, should see what is really going on here. So while Holder refuses to try to enforce laws regarding absentee ballots for the U.S. military men and women serving bravely overseas, he is focused on a tiny group of individuals who refuse to follow the rules.

Why he is suing States that are trying to protect the border is a mystery. I have my ideas…

How Irresponsible Can You Be

Talk about enabling irresponsibility! In the era we live in today of technology advancements made at lightning speed – it is mind boggling that anyone could survive a week or month without identification. Ever lose your wallet? Life stops until replacements are in place. In 2012, one can use a smartphone to video conference, check a bus schedule, make a dinner reservation, or check the balance on a bank account or EBT Card (Food stamps).

What better way to help someone? Look - If someone is that far down that they can't get it together enough to get id – the first step to helping that person would be to get them identification. With identification, maybe Social Services will allow the person to find a home, clean shower, a hot meal, or a job. Without ID … this person is locked in a box with no opportunity. As I said before, I really doubt there are that many individuals who are beaten down that badly that they don't have identification.

You cannot get a job or social services without identification. And if you don't have a job, then you have plenty of time to get identification. You cannot board a plane, train or (some) buses without identification. Getting medical care and/or prescription drugs for you or your children requires identification. And let's face it, you can order anything online – medications, education, and many other items that are much more sophisticated than identification. You can order a date or a bride online!

Some claim they are in rural areas, and would have to drive far distance to get an ID. Well, if you chose to live in a rural area, then you chose to have to drive a distance to do anything include voting! Your choice to live in a rural area means you chose to drive long distances for shopping, gasoline, doctors, movie theaters, roller skating rings, parks, etc. And yes…voting. We respect your choice to live in a rural area – but I shouldn't have to give up my vote because you chose to live in a rural area … should I?

I suggest that if you really, really cannot get your act together, and you don't have any other the items above (cell phone, lease, electric bill, EBT Card, etc.) then quite frankly, you probably have no desire to vote. Imagine what this person might say, "I live in a tree, forage off the land, no car, no utilities, no doctor, no public schooling … but I want to vote!" Not likely!

"I am unable to get an id"

just doesn't cut it in the year 2012.

How lame can you be?

Fix the Actual Problem

Rather than throw away my vote – fix the problem you state would cause "poor" to be unable to vote.

PASS A LAW THAT REQUIRES ALL STATES TO PROVIDE FREE STATE IDENTIFICATIONS.

The infrastructure is already in place! (Driver's licenses facilities)

Again, since we are talking about a miniscule number of people, wouldn't this make more sense? Isn't this better then disenfranchising my vote; and the votes of millions of U.S. citizens who follow the rules?

I sat down on the train – the same train I took home every day. The 5:10 PM from Penn Station to Babylon on the Long Island Railroad. I waved to the people I became accustom to seeing every day. Recently, a few minutes prior to the departure time, a guy would walk onto the train and announce that he was short $5 dollars for a ticket; couldn't anyone help him out as he just wanted to go home. Most ignored him, fumbling their newspapers or books. Certainly none of the regulars would fall for this ruse. After a few minutes, whether he collected a couple dollars or not, he would walk off the train. He went from train to train – saying the exact same story. One day, I decided to try something. Human nature is predictable – especially when you show someone – clearly – that you are aware *of their deception. Some will get mad! So when this guy finished his familiar plea – I spoke up, "Go ahead and sit down. When the ticket taker comes, I will give him the couple bucks you are short." His facial expression said what his mouth could not. He stood there – thinking about the predicament he was in. Everyone would know his story was bogus if he didn't sit down. He stormed off the train – as I received a resounding applause from the regulars. We never saw him again.*

This is what those who refuse to fix the REAL problem are doing!

So if they want to solve the problem, then why do they refuse to pass a law to provide ID to 100 or even 1000 people nationwide - who actually can prove that they have no identification. But if they have any of the items in the list above (cellular phone, bus pass, doctor, kids in school), they have identification.

Millions of dollars, scores of people, and months of time (full time) are being spent to steal U.S. elections. That's right – it would take less time, money, and effort to provide a limo ride, free photo at a camera store, and a free identification card!! Yet some are so determined to steal elections that they will spend many times more money and time – just to allow Donald Duck to vote!

No - this is about stealing elections by nullifying my cherished vote!

CHAPTER 10

WATERGATE II

Who would have accepted the Nixon Administration investigating itself during the Watergate scandal?

That was what the Nixon Administration told everyone it planned to do (initially) to investigate the issue back in 1973. Most of the U.S. press pounced saying that would be like a "fox investigating missing chickens", and demanded a real investigation. And rather than let Nixon investigate himself, an independent counsel was appointed the task. No one died in the Watergate scandal! No police officers or other law enforcement personnel were murdered. And had the Nixon Team been allowed to investigate itself, there is a good chance things would have turned out quite different. Hundreds of people *did not* die as a result of the Watergate scandal. In fact, no one was even injured.

Or what if the Nixon Team appointed a so called "independent prosecutor" - a person who contributed thousands of dollars to Nixon Administration officials – would that have been acceptable to you? More about leaks of critical national secrets later.

Johnny may have been only 7 years old, but he knew he was in trouble. His mom told him that dinner would be ready soon and he was not allowed to open the package of delicious chocolate chip cookies grandma baked and left on the kitchen counter. So when mom said she needed to walk up to the corner store "real quick for some half and half", he thought this was his opportunity! He could carefully open the package, pull out one small cookie and reseal the package. No one would know. Dad was in the Living Room watching the ball game on TV, so if he ran upstairs to his room, he'd be able to eat that scrumptious treat. This was a 7 year old with a plan! So as he is walking back to his bedroom, cookie in hand, one could imagine his face as he rounded the staircase, and walked right into his mom. "Mrs. Hantak loaned me some half and half – saved me a trip. Let me see your hands – do you need to wash up before supper?" Rut row! Houston we have a problem. Johnny had cleverly hid the cookie behind his back – Mom wasn't paying attention as she was thrilled to have the half and half. But now… now she was focused and wanted to see his hands. Like any 7 year old, he showed her the hand with no cookie and hope that would satisfy her. Being a mom, she was now sensing that Johnny was up to something. "Um hum… and what about the other hand John Junior?" Johnny's face said it all – mom knew he was being deceptive. Nevertheless, after showing one hand to his mom, he put that hand behind his back, switch the cookie to the other hand, and then showed the other hand to his mom – with a big smile. "See, all clean". Do you think that satisfied his mom?

Johnny was cleaver for his age – but his Mom was not going to let that go without saying, "Show me both hands". Is anyone shocked by this mom's action? Why not? Well obviously, if both Johnny's hands were clean, he would have offered them up without hesitation. Correct? It's logic that any attentive Mom or Dad becomes well versed in - by the time their child reaches the "age of reason". "You heard her son, show you mother both", said his Dad. Evidently Dad, who had been eavesdropping from the Living Room, caught on to the situation quickly. What Johnny didn't know was that his Dad had heard someone getting into the cookies a few minutes earlier. He put two and two together as he approached his son. "Your mother told you no cookies before dinner so put it back, wash up, and tell your sister that dinner is ready."

But how did he know Johnny had a cookie? It could have been anything… his sister's diary, a tool from the garage, a treat for the dog. How did he know it was a cookie? Did Dad have x-ray vision? More importantly, Johnny wondered how it was that both his parents knew he was hiding anything.

This is what DOJ head Eric Holder did regarding the deaths of hundreds of people. First he refused to testify completely about the disastrous plan implemented under his watch. Then he tried to say it was actually part of a similar "operation" started years before. When that was shown to be completely false, he simply refused to answer questions or provide the requested documents. Instead, he attempted to overwhelm Congress by providing a virtual library of documents – most unrelated to the investigation. In fact, most of the unrelated documents were not even requested by the congressional committee investigating the killing of over 300 people.

By showing only one hand to his Mom, it was a red flag to his parents that Johnny was caught doing something he shouldn't have been doing. After just a few minutes of analysis, his parents we correct to realize Johnny was sneaking a cookie.

When Holder asked Obama to sign an Executive Order shielding the DOJ from having to provide the requested information – well it confirmed to the world that Holder was indeed hiding facts that, if known, would cause his ouster – and possibly jail time if convicted. Just days earlier, he agreed to turn over the requested documents if, in return, the committee promised to not do anything if the documents showed crimes were committed. Can you imagine?

The Congressional committee already knew the answer – a brave whistle blower provided emails that showed the DOJ was involved in a major cover-up to shield the Obama Administration. Based on the info collected by the committee, and verified by the information provided by the whistleblowers, it appears that the real goal of the operation was to change gun laws in America.

And even more alarming is that it appears that the 300 plus people who died were considered "collateral damage" by the DOJ.

Brian Terry was one of those killed. He was a U.S. Border Patrol Office. It seems to me that Holder is, on the one hand, preventing states from securing the border, and at the same time he has some weird "social experiment" going on with guns. After refusing to cooperate with Congress, he convinced Obama to protect him and his team by blocking Congress's access to the information. With so much crime in America, isn't the DOJ supposed to be focused on that? Rather than sue states who in reality are stepping up for the Federal government that seems to have a "open borders" policy, maybe Holder should pay attention to Chicago and the daily slaughter happening there.

Had the Nixon Administration investigated itself during Watergate, well… what do you think would have happened?

Would any American have been satisfied if the Nixon Administration agreed to provide the requested info - BUT ONLY if investigators agreed beforehand not to hold anyone accountable if the information showed crimes were committed?

This is unbelievable!

When Nixon found out what was going on, he tried to shield the wrongdoers using the power of the office of President. By doing so, he became part of the cover-up. In my opinion, by signing an executive order preventing access to requested documents that are known to exist thanks to the whistleblowers, Obama is injecting himself into what appears to be a cover-up… just as Nixon did in 1973. This must be very bad – remember, no one died or was even hurt in the Watergate scandal. Hundreds of innocent people did not die in Watergate. This must be big!

What are they really hiding?

CHAPTER 11

LEAKS

Talk about a contrast! For years we have heard those on the left and in the press complain about the outing of a covert CIA operative, Valerie Plame during the Bush years. We heard how the leak took her out of the field, put her at risk from enemies, and was done as a "payback". An independent prosecutor was appointed, and VP aide Scooter Libby was tried and convicted (even though evidence later surfaced that showed he was never actually responsible for the leak). Remember?

Well consider this.

Shortly after being "outed", she wrote a book about the entire ordeal. That sounds a little odd if you are worried about enemies.

Then she appeared on TV promoting her book. Gosh, didn't she realize that now all the enemies know what she looks like? Do an Internet search on her name. To call her a covert spy is like calling Bill Clinton an expert at the Saxophone. And she certainly isn't hiding … not at all!

Maybe it's time Mrs. Plame had her own payback? She was very much unknown before this happened, and honestly couldn't sell a newsletter for her local PTA. Today, she self-promotes all over the web, she released a book, and her book did very well! Since Bush and Libby supposedly caused all this, shouldn't she share the book royalties with them?

The point is that the way things turned out, it seems hard to believe – that to this day, Bush is chastised for it in the press. No one died, millions in developed technology wasn't lost, and allies haven't lost faith in the USA. And to highlight the hypocrisy, those who complained the loudest about an obscure individual like Valerie Plame, completely dismiss the leaks and failures:

1. Drone technology flown to Iran
2. Helicopter stealth technology given to Pakistan (China North Korea, and Russia)
3. Israel plans to remove nuclear plant in Iran
4. Wiki-leaks
5. Which airbase Israel plans to use in a mission in Iran
6. Doctor who assisted the OBL raid in Pakistan
7. Details around Stuxnet and Flame - computer viruses that disrupt Iran's nuclear program

The most shocking leaks – the leaks that are treasonous are the leaks that started to come out in 2011 and 2012. They cost lives! And they destroyed operations in several countries. The initial reports said the leaks were directly from Cabinet level people in the Obama Administration.

And the Administration is blocking all efforts to determine who it was (even though we all know exactly who leaked and why they leaked.) Shameful! Prison is TOO GOOD!

Leaks put many covert operations in jeopardy, may cost additional lives because agents were "outed", and led to the Pakistani government sentencing a man to 30 years in prison. This man helped the U.S. over the years and gave information that helped validate bin Laden's location! Leaks helped Iran – they shifted their defenses once the Administration announced the route of attack on Iran's covert nuclear weapons program!

Leaks are bad – self-serving leaks are treasonous. To date, no one has been charged.

CHAPTER 12

RACE IN POLITICS

I don't remember anyone asking if it was a possibility that racism was behind criticisms of people like Former National Security Advisor and Secretary of State Condoleezza Rice, or former Ambassador and Congressman Andrew Young, or Former Secretary of State and Four Star General Colin Powell. I don't remember any of these leaders making claims or even implying that racism was behind criticism levied against them. I do not remember race even being an issue regarding these amazing, exceptional Americans leaders – who also happen to be black. Do you? Do you remember news anchors asking their guests whether they thought race was real reason for the relentless attacks on former Attorney General Alberto Gonzales or criticism from the right regarding Georgia Congressman and Civil

Rights Pioneer John Lewis? No – and even if some of the pundits tried to imply that if Condi or Alberto were white, the democrats would leave them alone – that was quickly dismissed. I remember Condi simply dismissing without hesitation, that her being a women or black were not the reasons for her critics. She said many times that her critics simply did not agree with her politics and that her race and/or gender had no impact.

And great leaders like Rice or Young (who also happen to be black) who proceeded todays class of politicians, avoided at all costs, resorting to claims of racism – even when there actually may have been a hint of it. They did so because they realized what the results would be! They realized it was a trap – a devastating trap that would have the result of slowing any gains made in race equality efforts. It's a trap that great black leaders who rose to fame in years past, like Young, Powell, Rice, Lewis, had the foresight to not fall into. It's a trap that recent leaders seem to be naïve to – and are even unaware that they are falling into the trap. Nothing could turn back the clock more than having a population that takes the approach: If you are going to cry "racism" every time someone disagrees with your politics or beliefs, then maybe you are not ready to be a leading black politician in America. Or even more destructive to equality would be to have a population that thinks that maybe, just maybe… America is not ready for a black president or vice president; because the public is simply unable or unprepared to respond to overuse of the claim of racism.

In this area, regardless of whether you agree with their politics, legendary and great leaders like Rice, Young, Powell, and Lewis were brilliant. The saw what happened when awesome leaders before them overused race each time opponents debated and or criticized them. Think about it. It is obvious to the public (in general) that it is not racism to object to, as an example, a road project – when in fact the person objected to the road project for 20 years regardless of the color of the person in office. Anyone paying attention quickly sees that race has nothing to do with the person's stance. In fact, it's insulting! Rice and Young saw these mistakes in the 1960s and 1970s – and they saw extraordinary people (who also happen to be black) go from being "rising stars" to those who fade away – because the color blind majority of the public is not interested in being accused of being a racist.

A friend of mine, Victor who lives in Chicago complained a couple years ago that he was being accused of racism by a few colleagues – because he debated an issue with them while having lunch in the cafeteria. His view was the opposite of one local black politician on how to deal with abandon buildings. He told me, "Alan – so my view has been consistent for over 30 years… never changed. Didn't matter what color the person on the other side of the table was to me… my view has always been the same! But now that I disagree with a politician that is black, in the view of colleagues who (obviously) do not know me very well, I am labeled a racist?" He went on to say that believe it or not – he was thinking about quitting after 15 years with the firm – everything was great until he disagreed with a politician (and also happens to be black). The thing is, Victor's wife (of 25 years) is an outstanding woman, wonderful mother, and ...also happens to be black.

Think about it. Pick any group or demographic you like. I have a friend who is gay. He will be the first to say that if a gay politician cries, "bias" or "homophobe" every time someone disagrees with the gay politician's views on issues, then the easy answer is to not elect gay politicians. Even worse would be a situation where gay politicians would be encouraged to keep the fact that they are gay quiet – because of the "negative connotation". Didn't we get past this decades ago? Talk about a step backward... come on folks, this is 2012 and not the 1940s! Other than like 1% of Americans that will never see their stupidity, didn't the rest of Americans proudly get past judging anyone based on color, gender, or sexual orientation? We did! To the ignorant 1% (or more like one tenth of 1%) who cling to bias long shed by Americans and most of the civilized world – I say it must be lonely under that rock!

Does anyone really believe that Holder was held in contempt because he is black? And if Holder was a white, Hispanic, or Asian man, that Congressional Hearings would not have happened? And does anyone really believe that if Holder wasn't black that the contempt vote would not have taken place? Or that if he wasn't black, the vote to hold him in contempt would have turned out differently? (Or by the way, that somehow – if The U.S. Attorney General was white, Hispanic, or Asian, that Americans would not care about voter fraud that dilutes their precious single vote?) I believe that if Holder was a "secret witness", with his appearance in the Congressional hearings hidden behind a curtain, and his voice altered… the outcome around all these issues, would be identical.

America IS ready for a black president. America IS ready for a black or Hispanic Attorney General… or Supreme Court Justice… or Secretary of State. America IS ready! Absolutely! If your answer to anyone who disagrees with you is baseless claims of "racism", then YOU are not ready for America!

America is not going to put up with law breaking, contempt or incompetence just because the person is not white. No way!

The U.S. media will ask if racism is the reason a republican disagrees with Obama on say healthcare or wants Holder to resign – even if that republican has never believed in socializing healthcare in America, and had the same objections for decades when debating others regardless of race.

But in 2012 when George Soros commits millions of dollars trying to make sure black republicans loose in the 2012 elections, no one questions whether racism is behind the efforts. I would like to know if Soros is spending millions trying to get any white republicans to loose in 2012. If not, is he spending millions to get only white democrats elected? I really do not know and have little interest in researching what Soros is doing. But since he has admitted to spending millions in the 2012 U.S. elections to get at least one black republican out of office, I certainly do have questions that the media is afraid to ask Soros:

1. Is he a U.S. Citizen? (he better be if he trying to change U.S. elections)
2. Did he earn billions investing “against” America and American companies since 2008?
3. Who monitors the content of TV and print ads he pays for to destroy black republicans?
4. What country is he from?
5. Is he okay with wealthy Americans influencing elections in his native country?
6. Does he pay more $$ to influence U.S. elections OR more $$ in U.S. taxes
7. If U.S. citizen, does he plan to renounce like other DNC supporters to avoid taxes?
8. Has he contributed to Obama’s campaign? How much?
9. Has he met with Obama or Secretary of the Treasury Tim Geithner? How many times?
10. Favors he got from democrats in return for contributions? (additional space on back)

But no one in the media will ask those questions.

In my opinion, to use race to build and/or protect your Legacy is the height of Hypocrisy!

CHAPTER 13

MEDIA

Why Americans need to GET A CLUE!

I could write an entire book on the hypocrisy of the U.S. Media. Others have already done so.

But because media collusion is critical to the creation and perpetuation of false Legacies, I feel it is necessary to cover the topic briefly. All Americans need to pay attention and see the truth about media bias! Believe me when I tell you that in the 2012 elections some uninformed Americans will actually vote under the mistaken belief that we are heading in the right direction. Since all recent data shows we are clearly not heading in the right direction, many Americans will make a mistake on Nov 4th. If the U.S. media was unbiased, they would report the truth! America is in the worst shape ever. The recession that started in late 2007, may have been brought on, in part, by the media in their attempt to frame the 4.5% unemployment as "terrible"! Over the last 3 ½ years the U.S. economy has not improved at all, and in some cases, has become many times worse than it was in 2008.

As I mentioned, I could easily fill an entire book listing examples of media bias and how this bias is why legacies, especially false legacies prevail. In fact, if the media in the U.S. was not biased, false legacies would never happen. I predict that the day will come, in the next decade, when the media is truly held accountable for "coning", "manipulating", and basically "flim-flaming" Americans. I am serious! Only when they are faced with either jail time or financial ruin (or both), will the U.S. media stop the lies so they can get their "guy/gal" elected to political office. And then once their "guy/gal" is in office, they protect him/her when he/she fails. Can you only imagine the reports if Bush had 3 years of unemployment above 8 %. Hey, I remember the media complaining about Bush's record on job creation back in late 2006 early 2007 saying that while 4.3% - 4.8% unemployment for over 2 years during the Bush 2nd term was "not too bad"; they implied that the jobs were not "quality" jobs. The media repeated, over and over, speeches by Hilary Clinton and Barak Obama complaining that the jobs were "low paying" and that 4.5% unemployment sounds low but that the rate was deceptive because they were not "skilled" jobs like engineers and subject matter experts in the sciences. (Obama would give his right arm to anyone who could tell him how to get unemployment down to 7%! Ironic isn't it?) The media replayed the claims so much that even reasonable people wondered if it was actually possible that America could do better… say 3% or even 2% unemployment? Was that possible? The media seem to think so. That same media, just a few years later, implies that chronic 8% unemployment is "…moving in the right direction." It's MIND BOGGELING to anyone with half a brain – to see the media cheer for 8% unemployment!

And the claim that the jobs (over 137 million) filled by Americans back in 2006 we low paying was completely FALSE! The USA didn't see before, and has not seen since - that level of consistent low unemployment, steady job growth, a higher quality of living, level of homeownership, and even a slight lowering of uninsured! NEVER! You must keep in mind a simply fact – when unemployment is below 5% for a long duration (like in 2005 – mid 2007), companies must compete for talent – and they will provide enhanced benefits like healthcare, retirement plans, education, and child care options. When unemployment is high for a prolonged period – the exact opposite happens. Companies pull back on benefits (1st to go is healthcare), pay / compensation, vacation time and even tuition reimbursement. No one really knows what will happen after such a long duration of above 8% unemployment – we are truly in unchartered territory. In fact, the prolonged downturn in the U.S, from mid-year 2007 to 2012 is now the primary reason the rest of the world is slowing and may go into recession after 2 years of solid growth. Obviously I am not talking about the dozen or so EURO based countries. They have their own issues and the fact is - the EURO based economies (combined) are relatively small and meaningless when discussing the global economy. China, Japan, Indonesia, Australia and even the eastern European countries have been doing very well over the last few years; while America has … lost our way.

Imagine if Reagan or one of the Bush presidents pardoned a friend whose family contributed millions to republicans and oh, I don't know … the Bush Presidential library. And, oh by the way, this friend was convicted of the largest tax fraud case (at the time) in NY, and then fled the country with the money. If this was a republican president, the headline would be …

Must be nice having an American President in your back pocket!

When Clinton pardoned Mark Rich on his last day in office – coincidently just hours after a White House visit from Mark Rich's wife Denise, I was sure the headline would read:

Rip off Americans for millions, flee the county, and invest stolen money wisely.

OR

Just buy your freedom back into the country – Another Friend of Bill Clinton!

Especially in a society that has an insatiable obsession with *anything* involving the famous and/or the "rich class" involving sex, greed, or even better - BOTH! So, of course, many of us were shocked by the absolute and complete silence in the U.S. media after the details came to light. International reporters held back nothing – some said it seemed obvious that his wife dropped off money, promised funding for his presidential library and possibly even had sex with Clinton – insisting that he pardon her husband THAT DAY so he could come back to the U.S. and enjoy the millions he stole from Americans. Some claimed the money he stole – was used in some legitimate businesses overseas that made Mark Rich a very wealthy man. And that the money he used to "buy" his freedom from prosecution was a tiny fraction of the wealth he acquired with the stolen money.

Since Mark Rich will never have to pay for his crimes, I really hope he starts giving interviews. He has nothing to lose and he may actually be able to sell a few books. I am sure plenty of Americans are curious how much his freedom actually cost – some say it was the equivalent of a "cup of coffee" to the average American. And now he can freely enjoy tens or even hundreds of millions of dollars right here in America! In my opinion, this is a direct result of having a "buddy" in the Whitehouse. Honestly, if George Bush did this, some U.S. News Networks would have 24 hour programing covering the story. There would be TV Shows entitled "X Number of Days with no Charges", "Bush's Pals and the Fleecing of America". Even my left leaning friends agree this would probably be the case. And if this was a friend of Bush, he would have been vilified in the media – forced to sneak around in disguise, hiding from public view like Casey Anthony. The media allowed OJ to regain some of his lost "hero" status again after his acquittal. But after Casey Anthony was found not guilty, and this is someone that may have really been wrongly charged by overzealous prosecutors, the media.... well lets' just say DON'T UNDERESTIMATE THE POWER OF THE MEDIA!

But Mark Rich is a friend and contributor to Bill (can do no wrong) Clinton, so you will never hear about this outrageous pardon! By the way, Denise Rich is a public figure as she is truly an awesome song writer. The U.S. media has never asked her (during the many interviews she has given) about the pardon. The U.S. media has never asked her about the Whitehouse "visit", funds she contributed to the Clinton Presidential Library in Arkansas, or how the millions of dollars stolen from Americans has made her and her family mega rich elitists. And in 12 years, she has given plenty of interviews – and if she were a Bush contributor everyone knows she would have been asked by now.

Most of the reporters in the U.S. media industry simply do not care how much the average American suffers. They may care when they enter the field, but once they have the "microphone", they use it to push their own beliefs and agenda. Prior to 2007, Sarah Palin was considered one of the strongest women in America. While she may not have been well known by the average public, and did not enjoy the late night social scene some politicians cherish, Palin was considered (across the board) an incredible woman. Democrats, Republicans, and Independents ALL agreed (prior to 2007) that if all American politicians were more like Palin, corruption, waste, and other excesses that are out of control - would cease to exist. She published the budget online! She forced oil companies to clean up and pay up! She changed the lives of average citizens, of all backgrounds, for the better. And no one ever could deny that! And before 2007, no one could image any reason the media would try so hard to destroy her with blatantly and calculate and planned attacks – Katie Couric's interview was absolutely disgusting! (Remember, Katie's job was to smile and read a teleprompter. She's admitted that there were plenty of times that she had no clue what she was reading – smile and read she was told!) People liked Couric because she was "chipper" and energetic. To do what she did …doomed her career. She was used and tossed. Today – where is she? Then there was the Charles Gibson's interview and attack… makes my blood boil! Other politicians spent thousands trying to dig up something on her – and all failed. When she was selected to be a Vice Presidential Candidate the media pounced! All agree that if Palin was a democrat – the media would have given her the credit her stellar record deserved.

Look at what the media did and continues to do to Palin! In my view, America needs a leader that will cut corruption, cut waste, and enrich American lives. America needs someone who will inspire business but end loopholes that actually cause companies to pay low or no taxes. Palin and others, who could actually help America, will make millions in the private sector rather than run for office! This "power" the media has today must be removed! In the same way that the paparazzi were, in a way, permitted to cause Princess Diana's death – things changed after that tragedy. I see that day coming in America, when news companies are held accountable.

Come on Americans – Wake UP!

You think it's a coincidence that almost all of the major News shows are hosted by Democrats? Some are former or disgraced politicians, some worked for the Clinton or Carter Administrations, some worked for Democrats in the House or Senate. Very few are independent. No one really believes that a former Bush spokesperson or Chief of Staff could later be considered "fair" as a news reporter. But no one questions George Stephanopoulos's position with ABC News? Not only was he the Clinton Administration's White House Communications Director, but also the Senior Advisor of Policy and Strategy for Clinton! Now he reports the news with no bias? Give me a break! No one questioned the impartiality of the show when Meet the Press was anchored by the late Tim Russet for years –all knew his background and his commitment to the Democratic Party.

What did Obama mean when he told Russia – that he'd do more after election? And why has the press agreed to not ask him this question before the 2012 elections?

And if you think the media is not important, let's have some fun! Take 30 seconds and fill in the following worksheet:

A. Storm name during Carter years ________________

B. Storm name during Reagan years ________________

C. Storm name during Bush Sr. years ________________

D. Storm name during Clinton years ________________

E. Storm name during Bush Jr. years ________________

F. Storm name during Obama years ________________

Did you leave A, D, and F blank? Of course you did – everyone does. And believe me, there were terrible storms during the terms of Carter, Clinton, and Obama. It's just that the media downplays storms when Democrats are president. Conversely, when Republicans are presidents, they hammer the president every chance they get. After the way the U.S. media reacted to Hurricanes Andrew and Katrina, one may have thought both storms were part of a diabolical scheme by Republican presidents to hurt poor people.

And not only did Bush create hurricane Katrina, but he steered the storm so that it only hit poor neighbors and skipped the wealthy neighborhoods. No one ever came right out and said it – but the media made it clear that in their opinion, Bush's Katrina was a racially motivated storm that Bush caused. Sound ridicules? Go research the online reports a few weeks after the storm hit – but prior to local corrupt officials' decision to allow federal assistance into the damaged areas. Funny - to this day, no has ever accused the local officials of racially motivated behavior, even though they are the reason FEMA and other agencies were forbidden to provide assistance for several weeks after Katrina hit the coastline! Bush had to threaten to declare martial law and was just days from invading Louisiana militarily – when local officials finally let the assistance in. Years later, the country found out the local officials were trying to protect their corruption and were willing to sacrifice the lives of a few dozen poor people to avoid jail. Do you think the U.S. media ever told the entire story? Do you think they reported the truth that Bush tried and tied, pleading and at times literally begging local and state officials to allow assistance – but was blocked? Not a chance. It is disgusting how the U.S. media continues to perpetuate the lie all these years later….

That is why most remember the storm names during Republican terms - the media pounds the names into Americans heads over and over….

Press reported in Bush years	Press ignoring in Obama years
$2.80 gasoline devastating	$3.50 a gallon is good news
Ignored 300k monthly jobs created	69k jobs - moving in the right direction
Food-stamps recipients drop by 500k	Food Stamps more than double to over 44 mil
Bush/Kennedy Seniors RX plan	RX shortages
Unemployment avg. 4.5% for 2 years	Unemployment > 8% for 4 years - all time record
Adding $4 trillion U.S. debt (8 years)	Obama adding $6 trillion (4 years) is fine
Extraordinary growth - small business	Boarded up stores under Obama
Water-boarding immoral	Obama drones killing families is moral
Deficit of > $500k one year	Deficits of over $1trillion every year
Un-insured not decreasing	Un-insured increasing to 51 million
137 million Americans employed	Americans employed decreasing year after year
4% to5% GDP is low	1% - 2% GDP is "improving"
Home Ownership – all time high	Foreclosure Rates – highest in decades

Hypocrisy is rampant…

The U.S. media spent so much time during the Bush years worried about freedoms, liberties, and privacy rights – specifically about eavesdropping on long distance phone calls. Even if the call was made to the Waziristan area of Pakistan (ruled by tribal leaders loyal to those plotting attacks on America). But oddly, the U.S. media seems enthusiastic about the use under the Obama Administration of spy drones in the USA - to spy on average Americans! And while talking about freedoms and liberties, the democrats want to shutdown talk radio! (Liberal stations fail. No sponsors see value advertising with them.) Yet the U.S. media tries to frame the argument as almost anything EXCEPT freedom of speech. I could go on and on…

Listen - do not minimize the power of the U.S. media. They pump data day after day after day into the homes of Americans. And much of it is true, but much of it is false. Does anyone honestly think that Rachael Maddow wouldn't have been strapping herself (in protest) to a tree if she were anywhere need the Hoover Dam when it was constructed? Now she's on TV promoting it. Come on, I like her but Rachael would be protesting the construction – worried about a threatened species of salomon, squirrels, algae or flee…

American's were told we should be fed up with 4% - 5% unemployment under Bush and wanted it lowered … but telling us (now) that it's lower at 8% - 9% is downright insulting. And we all remember when the number of Food Stamps recipients ticked up under Bush. The media made it clear that it was concerning … but since Obama took over, the number of people on Food Stamps has doubled – but that is not even news. Actually, the media seems to be pushing a strange concept for most Americans – the concept that going on food stamps is a good thing? Millions of taxpayer money is being wasted on TV ads to encourage senior citizens to enroll for food stamps. When I first heard the commercial I thought it was for a weight loss program, or maybe a company that helps people quit smoking. In fact, there are hints that this may be a little bit of Legacy Building in progress. I am beginning to wonder if we may hear, in a few years, that encouraging seniors to go on Food stamps was all part of the plan to improve senior's diets! Oh brother! The headline had this happened say 5 years ago – **Bush's answer is Food Stamps?**

Educated people are fully aware that while the democrats had a super majority in Congress (2008 – 2010) they passed, and Obama signed the first ever significant cut to Medicare. Democrats cut approximately 3/4 trillion dollars from Medicare and seniors will see their "out of pocket" payments soar and services cut. With so much less money available for other things like food, rent, and utilities – food stamps will fill the void created by Obama cuts to Medicare. Or so that is the "story" being sold. It really is a great solution when 100 – 200 Americans retire each week. However, and this is huge, when 10,000 or more senior citizens retire each week in America, as is the case today, this is a disaster in the making.

There are so many examples of media bias enabling false legacies! Earning millions of dollars every year is bad and you are part of the evil 1% crowd … unless you are an actor, athlete, or entertainer and you contribute to the DNC. Simple examples like:

Choice is good … unless it's about which school to send your child
Choice is good … unless it's about joining a corrupt union
Choice is good… unless it's about which doctor cares for your child
Choice is good… unless it's about college student loans

Even if there is no proof that humans cause global cooling / warming … "average people" should walk or ride a bicycle, so Alec Baldwin, Al Gore, and Pelosi can use limos and jets. Not me!

In the view of the U.S. media, Obama's campaign promise to reduce the annual deficit by 50% to $380 billion per year… is not inconsistent with the fact that he doubled it to $1.3 trillion. And it's not a news story worth reporting. Would it be during the Bush years? I would say yes since the media characterized Bush's annual deficits of $500 billion as very bad for America. In fact some in the U.S. media seem to suggest that we should not have responded to 9/11! Remember the claims of budget deficits caused by the "un funded" wars? But after seeing $1 trillion (or more) in annual deficits under the Obama Administration each year for 4 years - this is a "step in the right direction" according to the U.S. press.

Lastly, campaigning at a church or a church planned function is wrong … if you are a republican or independent politician. In that case, separation of church and state applies!

U.S. Credit Rating

What really highlights the bias of the U.S. media is the way they ignored the downgrade of the U.S. Credit Rating. This was shockingly bad - didn't even happen during the Carter years – and was ignored by the media. Had this happened during the Bush years, there would be special TV broadcasts, as well as themes and banners used every single night during the news. Think about the nicknames and slogans (and have a little fun):

- Duba Downgrade
- Downgrade? I thought he asked if I wanted Lemonade
- Standard and Poor's who?
- Bush's Downgrade
- Uncle Fed (First Ever Downgrade)
- It's the Downgrade Stupid!
- Downgrade = One Term
- Downgrade for Dummies Book
- Downgrade? W - You Are Fired!
- Final Straw for Americans – Downgrade (never before)

At Bain, Romney's only job – was to make money for the investors. Period!! The fact, that he helped create 100,000s of jobs – as a side effect – not bad! Obama's main goal should be to get the government out of the way so businesses can create jobs. IT IS Obama's job to ensure the government is not restricting business and to ensure the government is not creating an environment that causes American businesses to be less competitive in a global environment. So … Romney creates 100,000 of jobs (as a side effect), and Obama "tries" to create jobs and has a net loss of 100,000 of jobs.

Leading up to the election some networks have deciding to forget the facade and are showing the American people that they are firmly behind the democrats – CNN and MSNBC proudly show their support for Obama. Lately, CNN has been starting their nightly news saying they are going to cover politics. However, they then go on to bring up a negative issue about Romney, followed by a glowing story that shows Obama in a 100% positive light. And I don't expect that to change before Nov 6th 2012. There will be no reporting on any of the issues – the very critical issues that are crushing the middle class in America. There will be little or no reporting on:

- Economy
- Food stamps
- Boarded up stores
- Foreclosures
- Poverty
- Gas Prices
- Unprecedented reduction of middle class wealth!
- National Debt

And there are certainly no reports on the way America is being left way behind most other civilized nations. I could easily fill an entire book listing the bias and even how media bias helps build legacies - especially false legacies!

False legacies that - in some cases - will last forever!

END OF THE BOOK

This book is about Legacy Building and my hope is that after reading it and double checking my facts (of course you should – that is why I provided links and reference material), you will now have slightly more skepticism when hearing silly claims made by politicians and media.

Please review the Legacy Points list you created for a few presidents as part of the quick exercise in the Forward section above. Are you shocked? Will you question "odd" comments from politicians going forward?

If you'd like, email the list to alanisonthemove@gmail.com – I am curious how the legacy points you listed may line up with the narrative the U.S. Media would like you to believe – true or not. But more importantly did your list line up with the facts - the easily verifiable facts? Or were any of them in the "false legacy" column?

Now when you hear someone claim they balance budgets, or provided health insurance to millions if not billions of Americans… you can chuckle knowing that this is someone who could care less about facts … and someone who could care less that you know they are lying. This is someone actively following a well thought out plan to build a lasting Legacy of Success!

God Bless!

APPENDIX

Food stamps

Here are a couple different ways to view the U.S. Food Stamp data from SNAP which stands for (Supplemental Nutrition Assistance Program). It is worth pointing out that from Oct 2011 until Mar 2012, food-stamps skyrocket from 20.1 million to over 46 mil Americans receiving benefits!

Based on the rate of increase since October 2011, the number of Americans receiving Food Stamps is projected to exceed 51 million people by Nov 6th, 2012. This is an increase of 5 million people since the Mar 2012 report - an unbelievable jump of 5 million more people in only 7 months. And the Total Costs are skyrocketing! In only 5 months – the costs increased over 19% from October 2011 to March 2012! And since very few people are leaving the program, the Total Costs of the Food Stamp Program will be 4 to 5 times higher than the day Obama entered office. And the rate of people going into the program is accelerating over the last year, not decreasing!

Another observation is that, since 1975, the number of people in the program ranged:

- Good Economy – 17 million to 23 million
- Slow Economy – 25 million to 29 million

FACTS:

- There were **28.2 million** people in the program on Bush's last day as president.
- After 2 years with Obama in office, there were **40.3 million** Americans on food stamps.
- After 3 years in office, there were **44.7 million** Americans dependent on the program for food!

If projections are correct, and if by the end of 2012 there are 51 million Americans on the program, the program will have increased by more than 11 million people in the 3rd and 4th year of Obama's term alone!

Below is a more detailed breakdown of the number of Americans on Food Stamps since October 2010, as well as the unbelievable explosion in costs – all which is added to the annual deficit and the national debt!

This is an ***increase of more people*** than the total number of Americans that were in the program in 1972! Or looked at another way – an increase of 11 million people in 2011 and 2012 ALONE is the equivalent (about) of half the people in the program – on average for the last 30 years! How long will it take to reverse this explosive growth of Americans who need help buying food? No one knows.

Figure 1 – Americans on Food Stamps and Costs by year

Year	People	Avg Benefit per person	Total Benefits	All Other Costs	Total Costs
	--Thousands--	--Dollars--	----------Millions of Dollars----------		
1969	2,878	6.63	228.8	21.7	250.5
1970	4,340	10.55	549.7	27.2	576.9
1971	9,368	13.55	1,522.70	53.2	1,575.90
1972	11,109	13.48	1,797.30	69.4	1,866.70
1973	12,166	14.6	2,131.40	76	2,207.40
1974	12,862	17.61	2,718.30	119.2	2,837.50
1975	17,064	21.4	4,385.50	233.2	4,618.70
1976	18,549	23.93	5,326.50	359	5,685.50
1977	17,077	24.71	5,067.00	394	5,461.00
1978	16,001	26.77	5,139.20	380.5	5,519.70
1979	17,653	30.59	6,480.20	459.6	6,939.80
1980	21,082	34.47	8,720.90	485.6	9,206.50
1981	22,430	39.49	10,629.90	595.4	11,225.20
1982	21,717	39.17	10,208.30	628.4	10,836.70
1983	21,625	42.98	11,152.30	694.8	11,847.10
1984	20,854	42.74	10,696.10	882.6	11,578.80
1985	19,899	44.99	10,743.60	959.6	11,703.20

1986	19,429	45.49	10,605.20	1,033.20	11,638.40
1987	19,113	45.78	10,500.30	1,103.90	11,604.20
1988	18,645	49.83	11,149.10	1,167.70	12,316.80
1989	18,806	51.71	11,669.78	1,231.81	12,901.59
1990	20,049	58.78	14,142.79	1,304.47	15,447.26
1991	22,625	63.78	17,315.77	1,431.50	18,747.27
1992	25,407	68.57	20,905.68	1,556.66	22,462.34
1993	26,987	67.95	22,006.03	1,646.94	23,652.97
1994	27,474	69.00	22,748.58	1,744.87	24,493.45
1995	26,619	71.27	22,764.07	1,856.30	24,620.37
1996	25,543	73.21	22,440.11	1,890.88	24,330.99
1997	22,858	71.27	19,548.86	1,958.68	21,507.55
1998	19,791	71.12	16,890.49	2,097.84	18,988.32
1999	18,183	72.27	15,769.40	2,051.52	17,820.92
2000	17,194	72.62	14,983.32	2,070.70	17,054.02
2001	17,318	74.81	15,547.39	2,242.00	17,789.39
2002	19,096	79.67	18,256.20	2,380.82	20,637.02
2003	21,250	83.94	21,404.28	2,412.01	23,816.28
2004	23,811	86.16	24,618.89	2,480.14	27,099.03
2005	25,628	92.89	28,567.88	2,504.25	31,072.13
2006	26,549	94.75	30,187.35	2,715.74	32,903.09
2007	26,316	96.18	30,373.27	2,817.26	33,190.54
2008	28,223	102.19	34,608.40	3,031.31	37,639.71
2009	33,490	125.31	50,360.41	3,272.81	53,633.22
2010	40,302	133.79	64,702.76	3,593.06	68,295.82
2011	44,709	133.85	71,813.40	3,855.53	75,668.93

Below is a much more detailed breakdown of the number of Americans on Food Stamps for Fiscal Years 2011 and 2012, as well as the unbelievable explosion in costs – every dime of which is added to the annual deficit and the national debt!

Figure 2 – Number on Food Stamps and Cost Details

FY 2011 and FY2012

National Data Bank Version 8.2 PRELOAD - U.S. Summary 05/31/2012

Table 2: Supplemental Nutrition Assistance Program (Excludes Puerto Rico)

Fiscal Year and Month	Participation 1/		Benefit		State Administrative Expenses 3/	Nutrition Education 4/	E & T Administrative Cost	Other Costs 5/	Total Program Cost
	Household	Persons	Per Person	Cost 2/					
	---- Number ----		---- Dollars ----						
FY 2011									
Oct 2010	20,183,177	43,201,052	133.76	5,778,525,983	--	--	--	9,321,916	5,787,847,899
Nov 2010	20,404,895	43,596,084	133.29	5,810,737,592	--	--	--	9,321,916	5,820,059,508
Dec 2010	20,668,184	44,082,361	133.61	5,889,655,092	776,397,867	33,591,103	83,683,782	9,321,916	6,792,649,760
Jan 2011	20,748,799	44,187,874	132.81	5,868,438,404	--	--	--	9,321,916	5,877,760,320
Feb 2011	20,791,408	44,199,479	133.24	5,889,268,903	--	--	--	9,321,916	5,898,590,819
Mar 2011	21,045,909	44,587,275	134.21	5,983,950,234	749,761,862	82,227,118	65,316,294	9,321,916	6,890,577,424
Apr 2011	21,071,176	44,647,781	133.26	5,949,815,789	--	--	--	9,321,916	5,959,137,705
May 2011	21,435,915	45,410,683	134.80	6,121,457,837	--	--	--	9,321,916	6,130,779,753
Jun 2011	21,394,401	45,183,927	133.66	6,039,397,710	780,747,288	39,294,232	122,404,315	9,321,916	6,991,165,461
Jul 2011	21,458,822	45,345,473	134.25	6,087,831,755	--	--	--	9,321,916	6,097,153,671
Aug 2011	21,723,850	45,794,474	133.88	6,131,029,980	--	--	--	9,321,916	6,140,351,896
Sep 2011	21,938,820	46,268,250	135.37	6,263,293,265	796,177,512	188,878,466	24,860,468	9,321,924	7,282,531,635
Total	**21,072,113**	**44,708,726**	**133.85**	**71,813,402,544**	**3,103,084,529**	**343,990,919**	**296,264,859**	**111,863,000**	**75,668,605,851**
Total 6 Mon	**20,640,395**	**43,975,688**	**133.49**	**35,220,576,208**	**1,526,159,729**	**115,818,221**	**149,000,076**	**55,931,496**	**37,067,485,730**
FY 2012									
Oct 2011	21,969,100	46,224,775	134.89	6,235,245,690	--	--	--	11,219,166	6,246,464,856
Nov 2011	22,027,321	46,288,314	134.13	6,208,416,983	--	--	--	11,219,166	6,219,636,149
Dec 2011	22,162,774	46,514,155	133.68	6,218,225,504	737,928,399	76,288,879	79,311,196	11,219,166	7,122,973,144
Jan 2012	22,188,732	46,449,737	132.44	6,151,690,048	--	--	--	11,219,166	6,162,909,214
Feb 2012	22,155,432	46,326,287	132.98	6,160,521,756	--	--	--	11,219,166	6,171,740,922
Mar 2012	22,257,648	46,405,204	133.20	6,181,023,733	709,810,810	203,630,826	63,498,408	11,219,166	7,169,182,943
Apr 2012	--	--	--	--	--	--	--	--	--
May 2012	--	--	--	--	--	--	--	--	--
Jun 2012	--	--	--	--	--	--	--	--	--
Jul 2012	--	--	--	--	--	--	--	--	--
Aug 2012	--	--	--	--	--	--	--	--	--
Sep 2012	--	--	--	--	--	--	--	--	--
Total	**22,126,835**	**46,367,745**	**133.55**	**37,155,123,714**	**1,447,739,209**	**279,919,705**	**142,809,604**	**67,314,996**	**39,092,907,228**
Total 6 Mon	**22,126,835**	**46,367,745**	**133.55**	**37,155,123,714**	**1,447,739,209**	**279,919,705**	**142,809,604**	**67,314,996**	**39,092,907,228**

1. FNS-388 data. Totals are averaged.
2. FNS-388/250 data for FY 1992 and FNS-388/46 for FY 1993 and beyond. Starting April 2009, ARRA SNAP issuance was 15.27% of total issuance in FY 2009; 16.38% of total issuance in FY 2010; 16.55% of total issuance in FY 2011; 10.95% of total issuance in FY 2012.
3. SF-269/SF-425 data are reported quarterly.
4. Prior to FY 2011, Nutrition Education expenditures were included in State Administrative Expenses.
5. Includes Other Costs (e.g., Benefit and Retailer Redemption and Monitoring, Payment Accuracy, EBT Systems, Program Evaluation and Modernization, Program Access, Health and Nutrition Pilot Projects.)
6. Supplemental Nutrition Assistance Program (SNAP) formerly known as the Food Stamp Program (prior to FY 2009).

KDALL ToC FNS-$ SNAP-$ Schools NSLP-P NSLP-M NSLP-$ SBP-P SBP-M SBP-$ CCCDCH-$ CCC-

Ready

Figure 3 – Chart of Growth in the Food Stamps Program

Oct 2007 – Oct 2011

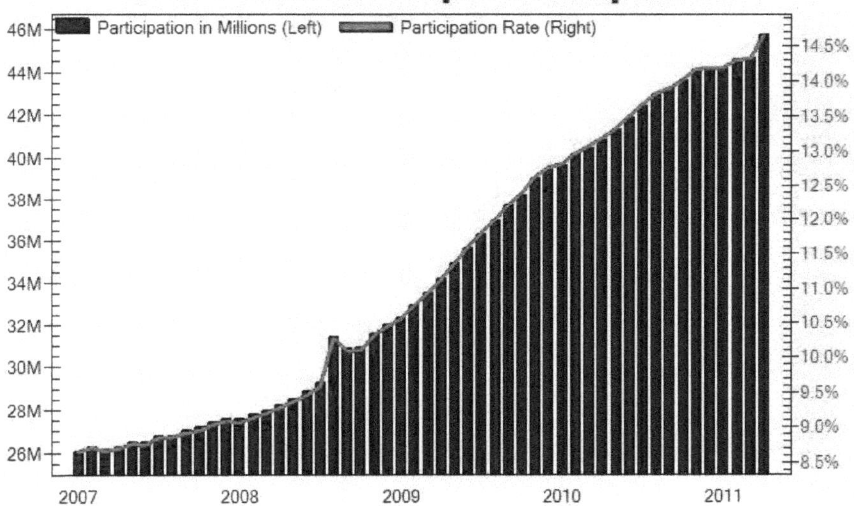

Unemployment and Employment

Figure 4 - Monthly Net New American Jobs

Year	Jan	Feb	Mar	Apr	May	Jun	Jul	Aug	Sep	Oct	Nov	Dec
1975	-360	-378	-270	-186	160	-104	249	386	78	303	144	338
1976	489	311	232	244	18	65	170	158	188	13	332	211
1977	244	295	404	339	359	399	348	238	458	262	379	235
1978	187	353	513	702	346	442	254	276	137	336	437	283
1979	137	243	426	-62	372	318	106	82	27	157	94	95
1980	131	79	112	-145	-431	-320	-263	260	113	280	256	195
1981	95	67	104	74	10	196	112	-36	-87	-100	-209	-278
1982	-327	-6	-129	-281	-45	-243	-343	-158	-181	-277	-124	-14
1983	225	-78	173	276	277	378	418	-308	1114	271	352	356
1984	447	479	275	363	308	379	312	241	311	286	349	127
1985	266	124	346	195	274	145	189	193	204	187	209	168
1986	123	107	93	188	125	-93	318	113	346	187	186	204
1987	171	232	249	338	227	171	346	170	229	492	231	294
1988	94	452	276	245	227	363	223	121	340	268	339	289
1989	262	258	192	173	118	117	39	47	249	111	277	95
1990	338	249	214	40	150	17	-40	-208	-85	-159	-146	-59
1991	-122	-302	-161	-212	-127	88	-48	17	32	12	-58	23
1992	50	-66	52	157	126	60	70	141	35	178	139	212
1993	310	242	-51	308	265	174	295	160	239	278	261	307
1994	270	201	462	353	333	313	364	298	355	208	422	272
1995	322	210	223	160	-16	232	79	272	244	146	149	132
1996	-21	434	264	160	323	279	232	197	219	243	296	168
1997	231	299	313	290	256	255	281	-16	507	339	300	300
1998	273	188	144	278	399	212	118	353	219	194	280	344

Year	Jan	Feb	Mar	Apr	May	Jun	Jul	Aug	Sep	Oct	Nov	Dec
1999	127	404	106	374	214	266	290	193	204	405	293	298
2000	248	122	471	288	224	-47	165	1	125	-12	227	136
2001	-15	63	-28	-282	-44	-128	-125	-155	-243	-331	-295	-178
2002	-129	-146	-24	-84	-9	47	-100	-11	-55	121	8	-163
2003	95	-159	-213	-49	-9	0	25	-45	109	197	14	119
2004	162	44	337	249	310	81	46	122	161	348	63	134
2005	137	240	141	360	170	243	374	193	66	80	334	160
2006	283	316	283	181	14	76	209	183	157	-9	204	171
2007	236	93	190	72	139	75	-40	-18	73	79	112	89
2008	41	-84	-95	-208	-190	-198	-210	-274	-432	-489	-803	-661
2009	-818	-724	-799	-692	-361	-482	-339	-231	-199	-202	-42	-171
2010	-40	-35	189	239	516	-167	-58	-51	-27	220	121	120
2011	110	220	246	251	54	84	96	85	202	112	157	223
2012	275	259	143	68	77(P)	80(P)						

Figure 5 - Unemployment Rate

(LNS14000000) Seasonally Adjusted, 16 years and over

Year	Jan	Feb	Mar	Apr	May	Jun	Jul	Aug	Sep	Oct	Nov	Dec
1975	8.1	8.1	8.6	8.8	9.0	8.8	8.6	8.4	8.4	8.4	8.3	8.2
1976	7.9	7.7	7.6	7.7	7.4	7.6	7.8	7.8	7.6	7.7	7.8	7.8
1977	7.5	7.6	7.4	7.2	7.0	7.2	6.9	7.0	6.8	6.8	6.8	6.4
1978	6.4	6.3	6.3	6.1	6.0	5.9	6.2	5.9	6.0	5.8	5.9	6.0
1979	5.9	5.9	5.8	5.8	5.6	5.7	5.7	6.0	5.9	6.0	5.9	6.0
1980	6.3	6.3	6.3	6.9	7.5	7.6	7.8	7.7	7.5	7.5	7.5	7.2
1981	7.5	7.4	7.4	7.2	7.5	7.5	7.2	7.4	7.6	7.9	8.3	8.5
1982	8.6	8.9	9.0	9.3	9.4	9.6	9.8	9.8	10.1	10.4	10.8	10.8
1983	10.4	10.4	10.3	10.2	10.1	10.1	9.4	9.5	9.2	8.8	8.5	8.3
1984	8.0	7.8	7.8	7.7	7.4	7.2	7.5	7.5	7.3	7.4	7.2	7.3
1985	7.3	7.2	7.2	7.3	7.2	7.4	7.4	7.1	7.1	7.1	7.0	7.0
1986	6.7	7.2	7.2	7.1	7.2	7.2	7.0	6.9	7.0	7.0	6.9	6.6
1987	6.6	6.6	6.6	6.3	6.3	6.2	6.1	6.0	5.9	6.0	5.8	5.7
1988	5.7	5.7	5.7	5.4	5.6	5.4	5.4	5.6	5.4	5.4	5.3	5.3
1989	5.4	5.2	5.0	5.2	5.2	5.3	5.2	5.2	5.3	5.3	5.4	5.4
1990	5.4	5.3	5.2	5.4	5.4	5.2	5.5	5.7	5.9	5.9	6.2	6.3
1991	6.4	6.6	6.8	6.7	6.9	6.9	6.8	6.9	6.9	7.0	7.0	7.3
1992	7.3	7.4	7.4	7.4	7.6	7.8	7.7	7.6	7.6	7.3	7.4	7.4
1993	7.3	7.1	7.0	7.1	7.1	7.0	6.9	6.8	6.7	6.8	6.6	6.5
1994	6.6	6.6	6.5	6.4	6.1	6.1	6.1	6.0	5.9	5.8	5.6	5.5
1995	5.6	5.4	5.4	5.8	5.6	5.6	5.7	5.7	5.6	5.5	5.6	5.6
1996	5.6	5.5	5.5	5.6	5.6	5.3	5.5	5.1	5.2	5.2	5.4	5.4
1997	5.3	5.2	5.2	5.1	4.9	5.0	4.9	4.8	4.9	4.7	4.6	4.7
1998	4.6	4.6	4.7	4.3	4.4	4.5	4.5	4.5	4.6	4.5	4.4	4.4

Year	Jan	Feb	Mar	Apr	May	Jun	Jul	Aug	Sep	Oct	Nov	Dec
1999	4.3	4.4	4.2	4.3	4.2	4.3	4.3	4.2	4.2	4.1	4.1	4.0
2000	4.0	4.1	4.0	3.8	4.0	4.0	4.0	4.1	3.9	3.9	3.9	3.9
2001	4.2	4.2	4.3	4.4	4.3	4.5	4.6	4.9	5.0	5.3	5.5	5.7
2002	5.7	5.7	5.7	5.9	5.8	5.8	5.8	5.7	5.7	5.7	5.9	6.0
2003	5.8	5.9	5.9	6.0	6.1	6.3	6.2	6.1	6.1	6.0	5.8	5.7
2004	5.7	5.6	5.8	5.6	5.6	5.6	5.5	5.4	5.4	5.5	5.4	5.4
2005	5.3	5.4	5.2	5.2	5.1	5.0	5.0	4.9	5.0	5.0	5.0	4.9
2006	4.7	4.8	4.7	4.7	4.6	4.6	4.7	4.7	4.5	4.4	4.5	4.4
2007	4.6	4.5	4.4	4.5	4.4	4.6	4.7	4.6	4.7	4.7	4.7	5.0
2008	5.0	4.9	5.1	5.0	5.4	5.6	5.8	6.1	6.1	6.5	6.8	7.3
2009	7.8	8.3	8.7	8.9	9.4	9.5	9.5	9.6	9.8	10.0	9.9	9.9
2010	9.7	9.8	9.8	9.9	9.6	9.4	9.5	9.6	9.5	9.5	9.8	9.4
2011	9.1	9.0	8.9	9.0	9.0	9.1	9.1	9.1	9.0	8.9	8.7	8.5
2012	8.3	8.3	8.2	8.1	8.2	8.2						

Figure 6 – Number Unemployed

(LNS13000000) Seasonally Adjusted, thousands, 16 years and over

Year	Jan	Feb	Mar	Apr	May	Jun	Jul	Aug	Sep	Oct	Nov	Dec
1975	7501	7520	7978	8210	8433	8220	8127	7928	7923	7897	7794	7744
1976	7534	7326	7230	7330	7053	7322	7490	7518	7380	7430	7620	7545
1977	7280	7443	7307	7059	6911	7134	6829	6925	6751	6763	6815	6386
1978	6489	6318	6337	6180	6127	6028	6309	6080	6125	5947	6077	6228
1979	6109	6173	6109	6069	5840	5959	5996	6320	6190	6296	6238	6325
1980	6683	6702	6729	7358	7984	8098	8363	8281	8021	8088	8023	7718
1981	8071	8051	7982	7869	8174	8098	7863	8036	8230	8646	9029	9267
1982	9397	9705	9895	10244	10335	10538	10849	10881	11217	11529	11938	12051
1983	11534	11545	11408	11268	11154	11246	10548	10623	10282	9887	9499	9331
1984	9008	8791	8746	8762	8456	8226	8537	8519	8367	8381	8198	8358
1985	8423	8321	8339	8395	8302	8460	8513	8196	8248	8298	8128	8138
1986	7795	8402	8383	8364	8439	8508	8319	8135	8310	8243	8159	7883
1987	7892	7865	7862	7542	7574	7398	7268	7261	7102	7227	7035	6936
1988	6953	6929	6876	6601	6779	6546	6605	6843	6604	6568	6537	6518
1989	6682	6359	6205	6468	6375	6577	6495	6511	6590	6630	6725	6667
1990	6752	6651	6598	6797	6742	6590	6922	7188	7368	7459	7764	7901
1991	8015	8265	8586	8439	8736	8692	8586	8666	8722	8842	8931	9198
1992	9283	9454	9460	9415	9744	10040	9850	9787	9781	9398	9565	9557
1993	9325	9183	9056	9110	9149	9121	8930	8763	8714	8750	8542	8477
1994	8630	8583	8470	8331	7915	7927	7946	7933	7734	7632	7375	7230
1995	7375	7187	7153	7645	7430	7427	7527	7484	7478	7328	7426	7423
1996	7491	7313	7318	7415	7423	7095	7337	6882	6979	7031	7236	7253
1997	7158	7102	7000	6873	6655	6799	6655	6608	6656	6454	6308	6476
1998	6368	6306	6422	5941	6047	6212	6259	6179	6300	6280	6100	6032
1999	5976	6111	5783	6004	5796	5951	6025	5838	5915	5778	5716	5653
2000	5708	5858	5733	5481	5758	5651	5747	5853	5625	5534	5639	5634
2001	6023	6089	6141	6271	6226	6484	6583	7042	7142	7694	8003	8258
2002	8182	8215	8304	8599	8399	8393	8390	8304	8251	8307	8520	8640
2003	8520	8618	8588	8842	8957	9266	9011	8896	8921	8732	8576	8317
2004	8370	8167	8491	8170	8212	8286	8136	7990	7927	8061	7932	7934
2005	7784	7980	7737	7672	7651	7524	7406	7345	7553	7453	7566	7279

Year	Jan	Feb	Mar	Apr	May	Jun	Jul	Aug	Sep	Oct	Nov	Dec
2006	7064	7184	7072	7120	6980	7001	7175	7091	6847	6727	6872	6762
2007	7116	6927	6731	6850	6766	6979	7149	7067	7170	7237	7240	7645
2008	7678	7491	7816	7631	8395	8578	8950	9450	9501	10083	10544	11299
2009	12049	12860	13389	13796	14505	14727	14646	14861	15012	15421	15227	15124
2010	14953	15039	15128	15221	14876	14517	14609	14735	14574	14636	15104	14393
2011	13919	13751	13628	13792	13892	14024	13908	13920	13897	13759	13323	13097
2012	12758	12806	12673	12500	12720	12749						

Figure 9 – Average Weeks Unemployed

Year	Jan	Feb	Mar	Apr	May	Jun	Jul	Aug	Sep	Oct	Nov	Dec
1975	10.7	11.7	11.8	12.9	13.4	15.3	15.0	15.6	16.1	15.4	16.6	16.5
1976	16.6	16.3	16.5	15.9	15.0	16.9	15.7	15.6	15.2	15.2	15.3	15.1
1977	15.2	14.7	14.5	14.4	14.9	14.4	14.3	13.9	14.0	13.7	13.6	13.6
1978	12.9	12.5	12.4	12.3	12.1	12.1	12.0	11.4	11.4	11.7	11.1	10.6
1979	11.1	11.2	11.7	11.0	11.1	10.4	10.3	10.6	10.5	10.5	10.6	10.8
1980	10.4	10.6	11.0	11.4	10.9	11.3	11.8	12.4	12.9	13.1	13.6	13.7
1981	14.3	14.1	14.0	13.9	13.6	13.7	13.8	14.4	13.6	13.5	13.1	13.1
1982	13.4	14.1	14.1	14.5	14.9	15.7	15.4	16.2	16.6	17.2	17.1	18.1
1983	19.4	19.2	19.4	19.5	20.5	20.8	21.2	20.0	20.2	20.2	19.7	19.2
1984	20.4	19.0	19.1	18.9	18.8	18.1	18.0	17.3	17.0	16.7	17.0	16.8
1985	15.9	15.9	16.1	16.4	15.3	15.5	15.5	15.3	15.3	15.3	15.7	15.1
1986	14.8	15.2	14.6	14.7	14.7	15.2	15.2	15.5	15.4	15.2	15.0	15.0
1987	14.9	14.7	14.9	14.8	14.9	14.9	14.2	14.4	14.2	14.0	14.0	14.2
1988	14.2	14.4	13.7	13.3	13.8	13.1	13.4	13.6	13.6	13.4	12.6	12.9
1989	12.6	12.4	12.3	12.5	12.0	11.1	11.8	11.4	11.5	11.9	11.7	11.6
1990	11.8	11.6	11.7	11.8	11.7	11.6	11.9	12.2	12.4	12.2	12.4	12.5
1991	12.2	12.7	12.9	13.5	12.9	13.7	13.8	13.9	14.0	14.4	14.8	15.4
1992	16.1	16.7	17.1	17.4	17.8	18.2	18.1	18.0	18.1	18.9	17.9	19.0
1993	18.3	18.2	17.6	17.6	17.5	17.8	17.7	18.0	18.1	18.1	18.6	18.3
1994	18.6	19.0	19.0	19.0	19.5	18.8	19.0	18.8	18.7	19.3	18.0	17.8
1995	17.1	17.0	17.3	17.6	17.0	15.9	16.5	16.2	16.2	16.0	16.4	16.3
1996	16.1	16.4	17.3	17.6	17.0	17.6	16.7	17.3	16.8	16.3	15.9	15.6
1997	16.0	15.8	15.5	15.6	15.4	15.5	16.4	16.0	15.9	16.1	15.4	15.9
1998	15.6	15.4	14.5	14.7	14.7	14.1	14.1	13.7	14.4	14.1	14.5	14.0
1999	13.4	13.8	13.4	13.3	13.4	14.3	13.6	13.1	13.1	13.3	12.9	12.9

Year	Jan	Feb	Mar	Apr	May	Jun	Jul	Aug	Sep	Oct	Nov	Dec
2000	13.1	12.6	12.7	12.4	12.6	12.3	13.4	12.9	12.2	12.7	12.4	12.5
2001	12.7	12.8	12.8	12.4	12.1	12.7	12.9	13.3	13.2	13.3	14.3	14.5
2002	14.7	15.0	15.4	16.3	16.8	16.9	16.9	16.5	17.6	17.8	17.6	18.5
2003	18.5	18.5	18.1	19.4	19.0	19.9	19.7	19.2	19.5	19.3	19.9	19.8
2004	19.9	20.1	19.8	19.6	19.8	20.5	18.8	18.8	19.4	19.5	19.7	19.4
2005	19.5	19.1	19.5	19.6	18.6	17.9	17.6	18.4	17.9	17.9	17.5	17.5
2006	16.9	17.8	17.1	16.7	17.1	16.6	17.1	17.1	17.1	16.3	16.2	16.1
2007	16.3	16.7	17.8	16.9	16.6	16.5	17.2	17.0	16.3	17.0	17.3	16.6
2008	17.4	16.9	16.5	16.9	16.6	17.1	17.0	17.7	18.7	20.0	18.9	19.9
2009	19.8	20.1	20.8	21.6	22.4	23.9	25.1	25.3	26.7	27.6	29.1	29.8
2010	30.3	29.8	31.4	33.1	33.9	34.5	33.7	33.6	33.5	34.3	34.2	34.9
2011	37.1	37.4	38.9	38.3	39.6	39.8	40.2	40.3	40.4	39.2	40.9	40.8
2012	40.1	40.0	39.4	39.1	39.7	39.9						

Figure 10 – Discouraged Workers

(LNU05026645), Not Seasonally Adjusted, Not in Labor Force, Searched For Work and Available, Discouraged Reasons For Not Currently Looking, Number in thousands, 16 years and over, Want a job now, Discouragement over job prospects (Persons who believe no job is available.)

Year	Jan	Feb	Mar	Apr	May	Jun	Jul	Aug	Sep	Oct	Nov	Dec	Annual
1994	600	489	533	502	436	532	542	489	521	460	447	445	500
1995	440	439	454	385	398	364	456	410	341	412	401	425	410
1996	409	455	451	403	352	414	423	415	391	374	346	334	397
1997	397	364	356	379	338	353	311	311	328	302	331	345	343
1998	374	361	343	344	268	311	374	280	317	333	310	358	331
1999	339	271	295	245	256	220	290	265	289	271	272	267	273
2000	236	267	258	331	280	309	266	203	253	232	236	269	262
2001	301	287	349	349	328	294	310	337	285	331	328	348	321
2002	328	375	330	320	414	342	405	378	392	359	385	403	369
2003	449	450	474	437	482	478	470	503	388	462	457	433	457
2004	432	484	514	492	476	478	504	534	412	429	392	442	466
2005	515	485	480	393	392	476	499	384	362	392	404	451	436
2006	396	386	451	381	323	481	428	448	325	331	349	274	381
2007	442	375	381	399	368	401	367	392	276	320	349	363	369
2008	467	396	401	412	400	420	461	381	467	484	608	642	462
2009	734	731	685	740	792	793	796	758	706	808	861	929	778
2010	1065	1204	994	1197	1083	1207	1185	1110	1209	1219	1282	1318	1173
2011	993	1020	921	989	822	982	1119	977	1037	967	1096	945	989
2012	1059	1006	865	968	830	821							

Figure 11 – Total Americans with Jobs

CES0000000001, Seasonally Adjusted, Total nonfarm, thousands

Year	Jan	Feb	Mar	Apr	May	Jun	Jul	Aug	Sep	Oct	Nov	Dec
1975	77297	76919	76649	76463	76623	76519	76768	77154	77232	77535	77679	78017
1976	78506	78817	79049	79293	79311	79376	79546	79704	79892	79905	80237	80448
1977	80692	80987	81391	81730	82089	82488	82836	83074	83532	83794	84173	84408
1978	84595	84948	85461	86163	86509	86951	87205	87481	87618	87954	88391	88674
1979	88811	89054	89480	89418	89790	90108	90214	90296	90323	90480	90574	90669
1980	90800	90879	90991	90846	90415	90095	89832	90092	90205	90485	90741	90936
1981	91031	91098	91202	91276	91286	91482	91594	91558	91471	91371	91162	90884
1982	90557	90551	90422	90141	90096	89853	89510	89352	89171	88894	88770	88756
1983	88981	88903	89076	89352	89629	90007	90425	90117	91231	91502	91854	92210
1984	92657	93136	93411	93774	94082	94461	94773	95014	95325	95611	95960	96087
1985	96353	96477	96823	97018	97292	97437	97626	97819	98023	98210	98419	98587
1986	98710	98817	98910	99098	99223	99130	99448	99561	99907	100094	100280	100484
1987	100655	100887	101136	101474	101701	101872	102218	102388	102617	103109	103340	103634
1988	103728	104180	104456	104701	104928	105291	105514	105635	105975	106243	106582	106871
1989	107133	107391	107583	107756	107874	107991	108030	108077	108326	108437	108714	108809
1990	109147	109396	109610	109650	109800	109817	109777	109569	109484	109325	109179	109120
1991	108998	108696	108535	108323	108196	108284	108236	108253	108285	108297	108239	108262
1992	108312	108246	108298	108455	108581	108641	108711	108852	108887	109065	109204	109416
1993	109726	109968	109917	110225	110490	110664	110959	111119	111358	111636	111897	112204
1994	112474	112675	113137	113490	113823	114136	114500	114798	115153	115361	115783	116055
1995	116377	116587	116810	116970	116954	117186	117265	117537	117781	117927	118076	118208
1996	118187	118621	118885	119045	119368	119647	119879	120076	120295	120538	120834	121002
1997	121233	121532	121845	122135	122391	122646	122927	122911	123418	123757	124057	124357
1998	124630	124818	124962	125240	125639	125851	125969	126322	126541	126735	127015	127359
1999	127486	127890	127996	128370	128584	128850	129140	129333	129537	129942	130235	130533
2000	130781	130903	131374	131662	131886	131839	132004	132005	132130	132118	132345	132481
2001	132466	132529	132501	132219	132175	132047	131922	131767	131524	131193	130898	130720
2002	130591	130445	130421	130337	130328	130375	130275	130264	130209	130330	130338	130175
2003	130270	130111	129898	129849	129840	129840	129865	129820	129929	130126	130140	130259
2004	130421	130465	130802	131051	131361	131442	131488	131610	131771	132119	132182	132316
2005	132453	132693	132834	133194	133364	133607	133981	134174	134240	134320	134654	134814
2006	135097	135413	135696	135877	135891	135967	136176	136359	136516	136507	136711	136882
2007	137118	137211	137401	137473	137612	137687	137647	137629	137702	137781	137893	137982
2008	138023	137939	137844	137636	137446	137248	137038	136764	136332	135843	135040	134379

Year	Jan	Feb	Mar	Apr	May	Jun	Jul	Aug	Sep	Oct	Nov	Dec
2009	133561	132837	132038	131346	130985	130503	130164	129933	129734	129532	129490	129319
2010	129279	129244	129433	129672	130188	130021	129963	129912	129885	130105	130226	130346
2011	130456	130676	130922	131173	131227	131311	131407	131492	131694	131806	131963	132186
2012	132461	132720	132863	132931	133008	133088						

DID I DO THAT?

Obama claims:

2008 – Knows what the economy needs

2009 – It was worse than anyone thought

2010 – Knows what the economy needs

2011 – It was worse than anyone thought

2012 – Knows what the economy needs

2013 - ?

Page left blank

ABOUT THE AUTHOR

It was awesome growing up in New York! It allowed me to see - firsthand - how such diverse people interact in a variety of ways. I also saw that if you put your heart in it – you can do almost anything!

In my teens, I learned that the basic problem with the two political parties in the U.S., is that each wanted the opposite from the Federal government. One party was a "tax and spend" party, the other party wanted to reduce the role of federal government to one task - national defense.

While attending Hofstra University, a friend and I went to a NY Rangers hockey game at Madison Square Garden in Manhattan. She was given free tickets to the game and we scraped up money for a couple roundtrip train tickets on the LIRR. Needless to say, neither of us had any money. So when a homeless person approached us while we waited for the train ride home, I had only the words of an idealist college kid to offer him; and I shared my philosophy with him until he walked away mumbling. He got an earful about how he could "be anything he wanted if he would just try… one day you could even be the president", I told him as he waved at me to go away.

In college, in addition to majoring in Computer Science and Mathematics, I studied the Soviet Union and even took a couple semesters of the Russian language. At that time, we assumed the countries that made up the Soviet Union would be trading partners with the U.S. once the Cold War ended! At that time, China was a closed society and didn't seem to want to trade with the rest of the world. Obviously, things changed! But in the process of preparing for a career that would likely entail regular contact with a society of people vastly different from the America, I learned quite a bit about the history of the Soviet Union.

Most who study the Soviets focus on the end result – corruption, fraud, two class healthcare, food shortages, RX shortages, and ultimately the collapse of the Soviet Union. But what I found fascinating was what led up to the "revolution" that formed the Soviet Union. What was the mindset of the people? Were they gullible? Why did they believe the speeches they heard that described a utopia society? Free healthcare and education for all they were told. Poverty would come to an end – Halleluiah! Paradise awaited and the communists had the plan. What disasters or harsh events led a relatively intelligent country - no, actually a continent of people to be led down an obviously hopeless path to disaster? All they wanted was a better life for themselves and their families.

With this background, I bring a healthy level of skepticism when politicians and/or the media are talking!

Since my college days, I have seen the U.S. press change! It evolved from being moderately bias, to be overtly ardent supporters, even cheerleaders who actually create the news – so their preferred politician can cite such news reports while giving speeches. "It's being reported today…" as though that prefix makes it a fact!

The process of Legacy Building or forming a legacy you desire while in office is something we have seen increase dramatically since Ronald Reagan was in office. All politicians since then aspire to have a legacy similar to that of Reagan's - a legacy of a strong, decisive, and intelligent leader who solved the nation's problems! Many disagreed with Reagan while he was in office. But no one could deny the incredible success of the Reagan Administration! So why wait? Legacy Building now begins years before leaving office…

This book is easy to read and understand. I will provide simple data that can only be interpreted one way. For example, here is a chart showing Monthly Jobs Created for the 3 years – 2001, 2002, and 2003. The data clearly shows the U.S. economy was in the tank (long before 9/11).

Year	Jan	Feb	Mar	Apr	May	Jun	Jul	Aug	Sep	Oct	Nov	Dec
2001	-15	63	-28	-282	-44	-128	-125	-155	-243	-331	-295	-178
2002	-129	-146	-24	-84	-9	47	-100	-11	-55	121	8	-163
2003	95	-159	-213	-49	-9	0	25	-45	109	197	14	119

Creative people will look at the data and bend their description to argue their case.

Whatever!

My intention is to quickly move through what would otherwise be boring numbers – and show how even the data above could be described as "roaring, with robust job growth" when paired with certain words or phrases. And if that's not enough, I will show

how, along with help from friends in the press, the legacy 20 years later could describe this data as the strongest U.S. economy ever!

With this foundation, we will then explore together some outrageously deceptive statements that are, in my opinion, evidence of Legacy Building in progress for the Obama Administration. Before the boxes were unpacked at the White House, the Obama team was already planting the seeds of a legacy of robust growth, low unemployment, and balanced budgets. Even before the U.S. unemployment rate crept above 7.8%, the Administration was working on a legacy of low unemployment with steady and consistent job growth (ignoring for the moment that it is consistently low job growth).

Many people my age remember how the U.S. press downplayed the creation of over 1.1 million new jobs in one month under Reagan in 1983! Can you imagine? Or the way many characterized the 24 straight months of unemployment below 5% in 2006 and 2007 under Bush as... terrible. But contrast that with the reporting when the press likes you – you're a success if only 89k jobs are created a month. Even if that is less than the number of Americans that went on disability the same month!

Phrases like "created or saved" have only one purpose – to allow a Legacy when the facts say otherwise!

The End

www.ingramcontent.com/pod-product-compliance
Lightning Source LLC
Chambersburg PA
CBHW030015290326
41934CB00005B/348

* 9 7 8 0 6 1 5 6 7 5 5 3 4 *